SURPLUS AT THE BORDER

For Ken Brown
and Cheryl Brown
our "oldest"
friends

Doug Remer

Surplus at the Border:

Mennonite Writing in Canada

Douglas Reimer

TURNSTONE PRESS

Turnstone Press
607-100 Arthur Street
Artspace Building
Winnipeg, MB
R3B 1H3 Canada
www.TurnstonePress.com

Turnstone Press gratefully acknowledges the assistance of The
Canada Council for the Arts, the Manitoba Arts Council, the Government of
Canada through the Book Publishing Industry Development Program
and the Government of Manitoba through the Department of Culture,
Heritage and Tourism, Arts Branch for our publishing activities.

 Canadä

The Canada Council | Le Conseil des Arts
for the Arts | du Canada

MANITOBA arts COUNCIL
CONSEIL DES DU MANITOBA

Cover design: Tétro Design
Interior design: Sharon Caseburg
Printed and bound in Canada by Friesens for Turnstone Press.

Excerpt from *Killing the Shamen* copyright Penumbra Press, Thomas Fiddler,
James R. Stevens. Used by permission. Translated by Doug Reimer.

National Library of Canada Cataloguing in Publication Data
Reimer, L. Douglas (Leigh Douglas), 1947-

      Surplus at the border: Mennonite writing in Canada / Douglas
Reimer.

Includes bibliographical references.

ISBN 0-88801-275-6

      1. Canadian literature (English)--Mennonite authors--History and
criticism. 2. Canadian literature (English)--20th century--History and
criticism. I. Title.

PS8089.5.M45R46 2002   C810.9'92287   C2002-903953-3
PR9188.2.M45R46 2002

*I dedicate this book to
my mother, Maria Reimer (Zacharias),
and my late father, John D. Reimer.*

Acknowledgements

First and foremost, I wish to thank David Arnason for his inspiration and support. I would also like to thank Dawne McCance, Dennis Cooley, Robert Kroetsch and Birk Sproxton, who read my original manuscript. Finally, thank you to Heidi Harms, Marty Reimer and Pat Sanders for their sensitive and helpful readings in the final stages.

Contents

Surplus at the Border

Introduction

Surplus at the Border:
Mennonite Writing in Canada

In the late 1970s, two Frenchmen, the philosopher Gilles Deleuze and the psychoanalyst Félix Guattari, developed a theory of minor literature useful for literary scholars. They argued that minor literature is written by a minority in another language not its own:

> A minor literature doesn't come from a minor language; it is rather that which a minority constructs within a major language. But the first characteristic of minor literature in any case is that in it language is affected with a high coefficient of deterritorialization. (*Kafka: Toward a Minor Literature* 30)

"Minor" means uncontrolled by the conventions of the major language in which minor literature writes. "Deterritorialization" means a group's loss of territory. This territory is not so much an actual space as a set of codes and rules that regulate behaviour. When the group experiences deterritorialization, its members find themselves no longer restricted by these codes, and when the group becomes reterritorialized, it reestablishes a new set of codes and regulations to which the group members are then bound.

3

Many minor literary groups clamour to be heard at the "borders" of the major group, in Canada's case, that group that speaks and writes English as its first and natural language. These minor groups, gathered around the outside edges of the major English group, I think of as an excess, as a busyness of immigration, as a wanting to "get in" by any means necessary, as a surplus at the border.

A "territory" is a social group that lives by a complex set of rules and codes, and for which each rule and code is crucial to its economic and spiritual survival. Disrupt these rules and interfere with these codes, and you interfere with the group's survival; you "deterritorialize" the group. Territory is, therefore, simply a complex set of rules and codes by which a society lives. All of what happens in that society is coded in such a way that the society works and functions smoothly. When traditions/territory/codes are disturbed in any one sector, then the whole collapses. Territory depends on belief; if belief in the codes fails at one spot (as in the classic story of the finger in the dike), the territory fails. So, courtship codes sustain a territory's economy; Sunday-as-a-sacred-day codes sustain its economy; the rules governing the domestic role of women (including gardening and pig slopping) sustain the territory's economy; specific baptism codes sustain the territory's economy; childbirth rituals sustain its economy; pacifism as a belief sustains its economy; communal pig butchering codes sustain its economy, and so on. In the case of Mennonites, these codes all sustained patriarchy (the individual male head of a family, not any group such as the church, determines the family's beliefs and behaviour) and were sustained by patriarchy. All of patriarchy's thousands of rituals, rules, and codes are Mennonite society's territory. They are its traditions. When these fail, in certain spots, or altogether, we can say the codes, the society, have been deterritorialized. It reterritorializes when some new system reorganizes the society around new codes and rules so it can function again. Territory is a socio-economic fact.

Mennonites form a territorial group with its historical roots in the teachings of the Dutch Anabaptist reformer Menno Simons (b. c. 1496). Simons believed that the "apostolic church pattern required the organization of individual congregations of renewed believers motivated by the Holy Spirit to lead lives of peace and service" (*Book of Fundamentals* 1539). Codes and regulations concerning peace, service, and church development govern the members of the Mennonite "territory" and become the subject matter of much of their literature.

Certain Mennonite writers have come to prominence on the Canadian scene during the last forty years. First is Rudy Wiebe, who has written many novels that speak for the Mennonite community. *Peace Shall Destroy Many* radically reterritorializes Mennonite Canadians with the idea that their own violence towards Aboriginal Canadians must cause them to reconsider their beliefs in pacifism. Readers of the novel—and many others, too, although only accidentally—come to understand that the institution of art is able to regroup a community threatened by the failing leadership of its religious, political, and educational institutions. Armin Wiebe, another Mennonite writer, has written three novels. His first, *The Salvation of Yasch Siemens,* speaks for the Mennonite community by reminding it of its irrepressible materiality. He reterritorializes Mennonites with a depiction of the community's appetites for sexual encounters and stories, for food and drink, and for the wild and burlesque. These material qualities combine to make southern Manitoba Mennonites a rollicking community, which suffers, however, from a debilitating tendency to pretend to a stifling, arid, hypocritical spirituality that it considers superior to life's pleasures.

The poems of Patrick Friesen speak with intelligence of the Mennonite need for a poet to lead them to self-understanding. Lyrical and material forces dramatically struggle in all his work. This struggle illustrates tensions in the European Mennonite intelligence that arrives arrogant and fearful in the new land with institutions and ideas already determined. Friesen's poetry describes the stubbornness of these same Mennonites, which resists the peace, humility, silence, and patience this new land requires of them if they hope to live here successfully. The poetry of Di Brandt takes Mennonites to task for not fulfilling the promise of love and pastoral pleasure for which Armin Wiebe's books have begun to commend them. She holds the group's leadership accountable for patriarchal neglect, and implies that love and vitality may one day return to Mennonite culture only when its institutions recognize and celebrate the value of its mothers and daughters. Sandra Birdsell's fiction—a number of exceptional novels and books of short stories—reterritorializes Mennonites with a vision of their alien, dysfunctional life in the new land. Love fails to cure the various neuroses of Birdsell's southern Manitoba Mennonites. Especially in the *Night Travellers* stories, possibilities for the relationship between Mennonites and Aboriginal people seem bleak. Unchanged, Mennonite consciousness will not be able to bridge the gap between the spirit of the native prairie landscape and the destructive traditions of Christian spirituality. Recent history has brought these five writers to prominence and they continue actively to write for their Mennonite communities.

Other writers, however, have lately come to public attention: John Weier, Lois Braun, Sarah Klassen, Delbert Plett, Miriam Toews, David Elias, David Bergen, Audrey Poetker, and Al Reimer. As their careers continue, these artists promise to develop into writers as important as the more established ones. They are worth keeping an eye out for since they will likely form the next wave of Mennonites whose ideas challenge the group to examine its political assumptions. A more complete account of their work and relative importance to Mennonite Canadians must be the subject of a future book.

1.

Deliberate Platitudes and the Extremely Alien Mennonite: More Recent Mennonite Writing

If I were writing a separate chapter on Delbert Plett, I would entitle it, "Deliberate Platitudes: Delbert Plett's *Sarah's Prairie*." I was asked some years ago why I thought the American Joseph W. Yoder's historical fiction *Rosanna of the Amish* (Herald, 1995) had sold as well as it had since it was first published in 1940 (375,000 copies). One way of thinking out an answer is to compare Yoder's novel to another Mennonite novel, Delbert F. Plett's *Sarah's Prairie* (Windflower Communications, 1995).

Rosanna of the Amish, set in Pennsylvania in the second half of the nineteenth century, tells the life story of an orphaned Irish Catholic girl adopted by an unmarried Amish Mennonite woman, who successfully raises her in the faith and traditions of the Mennonite Amish people. Rosanna resists pressures from members of her family to repudiate the Amish religion and to return to her Catholic roots, and triumphs over the forces of selfishness and change. This victory of the conservative and the good greatly satisfies the readership's appetite for heroic loyalty. *Sarah's Prairie* similarly tells the story of a sincere young Mennonite, regaling its readers with the quirky adventures of Martien Koep, son of Isebrandt and Liesabet Koep, son and daughter-in-law of

Sarah Koep, after whom a particular fictional region of the Mennonite East Reserve in Manitoba takes its name. Martien's life initially develops along less loyal and proper lines than Sarah's, but by the end of the novel, his newfound devotion and faith equal Sarah's in ardency and respectability. Martien, at first, rebels with a certain degree of local notoriety, then experiences conversion, and after a few trials of his faith, including a brief flirtation with the evangelical Morsavian church, thankfully adopts the humble "Old Laender" faith of his fathers.

If these two books have this faithfulness in common, why will Yoder's novel outsell Plett's one hundred times over in the course of their existence? I want to suggest two reasons. The obvious one is the style of writing. Yoder's writing flows and meanders like a brook through the *hortus conclusus* of our pastoral English minds. Its prose, sophisticated and suave, stands with one black polished boot up on a fireplace fender of some London Old Boys' Club, a languid, white-gloved hand dallying with a fine cigar. Yoder's text absolutely understands major English literary conventions. Plett's writing, on the other hand, everywhere betrays its "minor," non-English status. It deliberately misunderstands and presents itself as misunderstanding the complex conventions of the literature, which the British once assumed every subject in its commonwealth, and in the English-speaking world for that matter, would have fully incorporated. *Rosanna* says:

> Before he drifted off to sleep, he pondered the simple, efficient life of this plain woman. Again and again, the words "quiet simplicity, peace, and contentment" floated through his mind. What a supper! What cleanliness! What piety! What freedom from strife and rivalry! And what joy and gladness Rosanna showed in obeying Elizabeth's every wish! (71)

Compare this now with a passage from *Sarah's Prairie*.

> It still shuddered Martien to think about that day. He remembered how scared he had been: Zoop Zak was lying in the coffin so still and white and all dressed up in his pin-striped soakj suit. There was the smell of formaldehyde embalming-fluid which they were just starting to use at the time. The substance created a distinctive odour of death which nauseated Martien even years later. It was awful to

think that the Morsavians in Salem were saying that Zoop Zak had died in a state of unrepentance and would have to spend eternity in the lake of fire. (36-37)

The latter paragraph flouts all the conventions of English literary learning: it inserts non-English words into the English text; it employs awkward verbs, being inattentive to careful choice, because careful choice subverts its purposes; it introduces into sadness the worst, least uplifting information (one avoids speaking of formaldehyde in a description of funerals if writing serious English fiction); it allows very funny names for characters, and in this funeral context, humour disturbs the peace that serious English fiction would attempt to achieve, like a preacher at such a funeral himself would strive to deliver.

All English literature's technology combines to create Yoder's passage. See here the standards of classical English literature and rhetoric, inherited from the whole history of Greek and Roman writing: well-chosen verbs, effortlessly appropriate to the tone and intent of the passage; varied sentence structure to keep the prose alive and pleasing; a series of persuasive exclamatory statements that decorously coerce the reader's emotional agreement with the author's *sententiae* about Rosanna's refined obedience. Every possible resource of language—all of language's subtle powers—is engaged to deliver a message. Such a marriage of language and message we might call the "major" imagination.

Plett's linguistic imagination is "minor." Exactly the "minor," Gilles Deleuze argues, effectively brings about change in language and literature. The major actually hates change and prefers always to pretend to endorse change while resisting it with a hold on the permanent as tenacious as a drowning girl's grip on her lifeguard's arms and legs. No, the minor is that which, by one means or another, forces major language to examine its own assumptions and agendas and to reluctantly change how it thinks about the (moral) universe. Deleuze says the power of the minor creates slowly, imperceptibly; it grows like grass within the boundaries of the major (*Kafka: Toward a Minor Literature*). The minor (Plett's novel) rebels, disturbs, stomps roughshod over the sacred, refuses to understand the accepted conventions of major language and literature, and all in all makes so many *faux pas* in its imitation of major language that it forces the unspoken

9

assumptions of the major language (for our purposes, English) to take centre stage.

Both novels have much going for them. Yoder's, with its smooth and official English tone, presents the reader with a world as peaceful and secure as can be imagined. Plett's, raucous and raw, undaunted by conventions of propriety in literature, disturbs the reader at every turn. Plett's strength lies in his ability to disturb and still entertain; Yoder's lies in his great mastery of literary style and moral appropriateness. Yoder's book has sold hundreds of thousands of copies. Plett's will be lucky to sell two thousand. Why? The reading world does not like to be disturbed, nor to have what it considers serious subverted any more than absolutely necessary for the sake of interesting narrative. It longs for, pays for, an affirmation of permanence, hope, love, and faith of a pure sort.

Much Mennonite writing of the late twentieth century belongs to the tradition of major literature, or "lyrical" literature. Its interests essentially coincide with those of canonized English literature studied in the academy: Spenser, Marlowe, Shakespeare, Donne, Milton, Wordsworth, Tennyson, Eliot, Hemingway, and so on. Its interests, lyrical rather than material, emulate the anti-communal, individualist, humanist interests cultivated by major English literature over the last five hundred years: essentially, the lyrical might be said to be the "official." It represents, whether it likes to admit it or not, the institutional (ecclesiastical, academic, legislative, artistic, military), authority and power, the establishment, the morally applauded, the unified, the undisturbing. An aesthetic of "secrecy" primarily *(for sure nich jevrich*—not generous) characterizes lyrical literature. One has to be an initiate to read lyrical literature well, to master it. Although it would appear as if a dominant society would not restrict access to its codes, that is precisely what does happen. A lengthy dominance of various societies by one society means that that society privileges its own million conventions regarding the reading of its texts and the moral systems built into its political and social structure. The requirement of a long and arduous training, for the individuals of the dominant society, to master its conventions means that these conventions provide much meaning and purpose, usually of a hierarchical sort, a sort requiring belief, and which bind individuals firmly to the official purposes of that culture. What is meaningless then is made meaningful in a dominant society; in the West such meaning is created lyrically. Instead of things being void of meaning, things are given meaning by these conventions. The void becomes, thus, meaning itself. Secrecy and initiation rites indicate the dominance of a culture because they mean that not everyone may understand its conventions of reading. Understanding is belonging; it comes with the requirement that the one understanding believe in the meanings conventions silently speak. One must be a sort of linguistic Mason in order to belong to the major, the lyrical club. Minor literature, on the other hand, non-lyrical by method, and so not secretive or elitist—though never to be mistaken for non-artistic or non-intellectual—operates via openness. It writes by an aesthetic of excess (often accidentally, thinking it is being deliberately and successfully lyrical). Much more of this "secrecy/openness" might be said at another time. Right now let it be enough to list those Mennonite writers who have imitated the major to the best of their abilities: Di Brandt, Pat Friesen, Sarah Klassen, Lois Braun, Sandra Birdsell, Rudy Wiebe, and others. Writers such as John Weier, Al Reimer, Armin Wiebe (especially in the first half of *The Salvation of Yasch Siemens*), and Delbert Plett belong to the minor literary tradition that celebrates, via excess, a material, bodily being, a being concerned only materially with moral, spiritual questions (the moral being an official interest).

David Bergen, a Winnipeg schoolteacher, has made a name for himself in the last ten years, publishing a book of short stories (*Sitting Opposite My Brother,* Turnstone Press, 1993) and two novels (*A Year of Lesser,* HarperCollins, 1996; *See the Child,* HarperFlamingoCanada, 1999). Bergen reterritorializes Mennonites with the idea that their old approaches to life are wanting. The new generation of Mennonites carries the same strong drive to be true to principles, but principles vastly other than those of the "territory." The new Mennonite territory imagined by Bergen is non-patriarchal. Di Brandt has already laid the groundwork for this place with her challenges to Mennonite male authority, and Bergen shows the new non-patriarchal male in action. The narrative elements in all Bergen's works are similar and the short stories neatly lend themselves to an analysis of his reterritorializing vision.

In the reterritorialized Mennonite community that Bergen's fiction creates, men live subjected to their wives and other women about them. Though wise and sensitive, these men keep their refined understandings and thoughts largely to themselves for fear of upsetting women. They live lives of high secrecy. Though never explicitly stated as being what motivates his characters, Bergen's men fear to lead; women make the practical decisions. Bergen's new Mennonite males are aesthetes unfamiliar with the world outside their own intensely self-analytical, inward one. Though Bergen likely does not think of himself as a pioneer of new Mennonite territory, the profile of the new Mennonite he draws tells us the story above. And his view of the new territory can be more clearly seen by looking at the relationship between his style and his subject matter.

Bergen's fiction tends to create male protagonists alienated in the extreme from their Mennonite roots. The story "The Fall" illustrates this alienation. It is a story in which the narrator's elderly parents, Mennonite immigrants from Russia and Switzerland, are, in their religious traditions, entirely unable to understand the horrors of the modern-day dysfunctional family.

> My father always thought that my daughter's illness was the wage of some deep-rooted sin, certainly unrepented and probably lascivious, perhaps Candace's and my living together before marriage, or Candace's leaving me just during the months when Anna began to throw knives at her parents. (*Sitting Opposite My Brother* 67)

The elders know little of the young couple's continuing terror, waking at night to try to calm their daughter, whose mental illness sends her into regular, unpredictable rages against them and herself. The parents, especially the father, agonize nightly while the old Swiss Mennonite grandparents pray in calm ignorance at home. The grandparents represent a failed Mennonitism no longer governed by codes that have any bearing on the problems of its late-twentieth-century membership.

Bergen gives Mennonites a picture of their world in transition after all their institutions have failed to operate effectively and the community is in collapse. A future, effective, Mennonite parentage will come to pass, partly as a result of Bergen's vision of the community, but he does not give us a view of that community in his writing. As in the story above about the Swiss Mennonite grandparents, many of Bergen's alienated Mennonite protagonists act dispassionately. Not only do they distrust Him, but they show indifference to the concept of "God." They love very little in their lives except the few children they raise inadequately, and the women they strongly notice on all sides and over whom they obsess. History holds no interest for them and they live unaware of political, religious, or social events. They seem weary of it all. Bodily senses may well exist in them—we assume they do—but not as far as any reader of the texts would be able to make out. When it comes to food, for instance, and the joys of cooking, drink alone (drink being Escape, of course, with a capital E) elicits narrative passions, not unlike in Hemingway's fiction.

> I realize that I'm still holding my glass and that the liquor is untouched. Maybe it should stay that way, but then the glass will stay full and I can see at the bottom way down there an angel, its image warping up at me, and I need to rescue that angel, even though it's a hundred miles away. (*Brother* 14)

"Let me drink, drink, drink, and be personally responsible for the safety of all the women in the world," this text says. Busy, diversified living holds no mystery or interest for this sad man, nor for any of Bergen's main male characters; they are each the walking cadaver as hero.

Bergen's subject matter determines his style. How interesting to see the current *zeitgeist*—the popular interest in all things extreme (extreme racing, extreme trucks, extreme survival, extreme mountain climbing, extreme dancing)—find its way into the style of a Mennonite writer engaged in writing the great American-Canadian novel. By "great" I mean what all uses of the word "great" applied to fiction mean: the first-rate, unique, and entertaining utilization of the conventions of realism to create a work of fiction with a significant theme. That is, elements such as character development, plot development, setting, symbolism, point of view, and irony cooperate to establish the heroic uniqueness and worth of a male protagonist. These elements create, in other words (and this is the mandate of modernist writing), a supreme individual of determined independence from social rules and codes, from the codifications of his habitus. "Great" literature in the twentieth century, in order to be great, must increasingly imagine the better loner, the better individual, the better rebel, the better lost soul, the better maverick. That is, in the "great" novel, some male's inner being must be examined, explained, analyzed, and presented in such a way that he appears more precisely representative of spiritually alienated Western "man" than all the fictional heroes who have preceded him.

The statement above implies that the history of realist narrative is the teleology of alienation. Successive works have almost knocked themselves out competing with antecedent "great" works in presenting alienation, until in the nineties "great literature" gets "extreme" (in the colloquial sense) alienation in realism (I am not talking about the genres of fantasy, romance, detective fiction, and others, but only realist fiction, the "grande dame" of the American-British-Canadian literary canon) such as Bergen effectively presents in his three works.

Subject matter determines the essential style of David Bergen's writing. In *Sitting Opposite My Brother*'s "The Bottom of the Glass," the narrator wonders how to speak to his wife.

> I attempt to explain all this to Vange but she has little patience for theories involving alcohol. She wonders how long I will go on using the glass as my way of mourning. And me, I don't know. I want to tell her that she, Vange, has always been my salvation, but that would be admitting that these days she's not enough. (9)

In this passage, as in many of his works, Bergen gives the reader a downhearted, uxorious, self-analytical male with not quite enough courage to tell his wife that he depends on her beyond the usual limits of human relationships. Such uncertain maleness is common in Bergen's fictional worlds. Look, for instance, at the appetite for the male to not be male in the book's title story.

> I plucked again at Bea's tights. The light from the fire rounded her thighs, and I thought how lucky women were, to be able to wear pumps and panties and bras and lipstick and four

earrings in one ear and short skirts and long flowing skirts.
Skirts: the word conjured up for me a world of mystery and
secrets. Men had such limited options. (91)

Ostensibly an acceptable transvestite inclination in the speaker, his real motive is snivelling weakness. He is a puling thirtyish
adolescent led around by the nose, unable to act but only to agonize (isn't agonizing always a sign of extreme self-promotion?).
This story's development depends on a pyschologizing protagonist named Thomas, who realizes his own inadequacy to deal
with his missionary brother's self-righteousness and complex
simplicity. Uncertainty forces Thomas to make the foolish-wise
decision to forgive the brother who has hurt him so many times.

> I lay beside my wife and tried not to think of him. I put my
> hand on Bea's crotch and left it there. I lay back and remem-
> bered how, as a boy, after fighting with Timothy, I'd lie in my
> bed and I'd cry quietly to myself and wish terrible things on
> him. Often, what I wished for was that Timothy's big ears
> would grow even bigger, grow and grow until they'd become
> so heavy they'd break his neck. (95)

The narrator despises his brother's religious fervour and
broods at length over past wrongs suffered at Timothy's hands.
But Bergen knows that a realist protagonist, despite his agnosti-
cism, must forgive where he is tempted to hate. So, with his hand
(extremely) on his "God's" crotch, he announces a sardonic forgiveness at the climax of the story:

> Now, in the dark, I smiled at that [the growing ears]. Then I
> leaned forward and began to whisper in Bea's sleeping ear.
> "Dream a dream," I said. "Dream that my brother's ears are
> growing and that with them he learns to fly. Dream that he
> takes off from this earthly vale and that he leaves us and
> ascends to heaven where he's always wanted to go. Dream that
> dream," I said. (95)

The unlikelihood of change in the protagonist acts as the
story's ruling irony (irony being the mainstay of literary adoles-
cence). Thoroughly ironic in his outlook, an extremist in his cynical knowledge of his own cynicism, the exhausted Thomas
knows more than his "traditional" (territorial) brother. He knows

more and better than his wife, whom he adores. He knows more and better than his neighbour's wife, whom he adores, too. He knows more and better than his brother's wife June, whom he adores and would like to love. He knows more and better than everyone that the beautiful mystery of women remains the only thing of value left in a valueless world. He feels the impossibility of joy, except as briefly made possible in directionless relations with women, and he understands the value of reducing the public awareness of his own cynical knowledge in order to stay in the good books of the women he adores and wishes to spend much time close to. (The reverse is never true, that women wish to spend much time with him, with the exception of an instance in his novel *A Year of Lesser*, because in realist fiction women must not love but be loved, even when they seem in the development of the narrative to be in a state of loving men.) Uxoriousness as joy (salvation) is thoroughly modernist and lyrical. Eliot taught precisely this: the inhabitants of the Waste Land have forgotten how to see God and how to think joy and have turned instead to sex. Bergen's and Eliot's views differ slightly, however, for one, in that the former imagines an extreme alienationist narrator. Bergen assumes that the knowledge of the alienated protagonist need not be an ironic, secret theme of the writer but the very *modus operandi* of all of a work's narrative elements.

Under similar narrative conditions of the exhausted, self-absorbed, mirror-gazing protagonist, all of Bergen's fiction proceeds to date. Despite the *apparent* subject matter of prematurely dead children, mad brothers, philandering neighbour wives, suffering fathers, and exhausted men wanting to know about the spark of eternity of a soul they think they have but cannot locate or find the energy to examine with sincerity, the *real* subject matter is something else altogether. The style in all of Bergen's writing, as I said at the beginning of this argument, is its subject matter. In each story, a witty, smart, observant, humane male spends his time utterly preoccupied with relationships. The main relationship that concerns him is his own with himself. The next type of persistent interest for him is his relationships with women. In sum, Bergen relentlessly presents obsessively inward-looking, bland narrators not immediately interesting to that reader who hopes for a rich historical-social landscape. Put another way, a reader hoping for an appealing mind at work on the world stage will not get that from Bergen who, in his seriousness, chooses (not unlike Beckett) to shun engaging material. What Bergen deliberately chooses to give the reader instead of the interesting is the lyrical "me"; the "I" looking in the mirror; the double; the *mise en abyme*; the "me, myself, and I" character whom almost all serious writers of "great" fiction have been preoccupied with in Canadian literature and abroad in the twentieth century (the autobiographical "I" barely veiled behind a fictitious identity. No history, no tales, no glory of other people, no knowledge of the philosophy of various interesting disciplines in these pages).

Bergen's narrators are the Freudians whom Valentine N. Volosinov, a turn-of-the-century Russian social theorist, criticizes in *Freudianism*, a fine refutation of the assumption of the superior value of the Freudian "self." The least interesting or productive preoccupation for a writer, Volosinov argues, is the personal interior. Such an interior narrator is exhausted with life, irritated with others and life, desiring only self-improvement, and expectant with hope for meaning, illogically derivable somehow from a steady look inside where clearly nothing exists (nothing is supposed to produce something *ex nihilo* in this narrative model). Not finding anything meaningful in the material universe is not the text's highest irony anymore. That climactic discovery ended as a literary argument *de force* some time in the first three quarters of the last century. Not finding anything inside has become the most ordinary everydayness of the realist narrative's point of view, of the narrative's progress itself. "Nothing inside" has been de-elevated in the teleology of alienationist narrative from its former prominent ironic, thematic status to the *modus operandi* of point of view.

Writer Al Reimer reterritorializes by giving the reader what Volosinov approved of as being more vital than a psychological hero. Reimer provides a strong material sense of the social codes that kept the old Mennonite community in Russia alive. He wrote his epic historical novel of the Mennonite experience while he was a professor of English at the University of Winnipeg. *My Harp is Turned to Mourning* tells the story of the Fast family's hundred-and-twenty-year sojourn in southern Russia. It presents, episodically, the story of ancestor Fast's arrival on the steppes in 1805, the conflict between brothers Wilhelm and Nikolai Fast, who end up in opposite armies during the Bolshevik Revolution, the long revenge of the rebel Makhno, who slaughters thousands of Mennonites, some of whom once employed him, and finally, after a long account of war and mayhem, it ends with the peaceful conclusion of Wilhelm's "journey" in rural Saskatchewan in 1933. In Canada, though he is a farmer, against his personal instincts, he makes happy use of his newfound freedom to draw and paint in the profession he had trained for before war and feuding ended his artistic dreams.

Where Bergen chooses to reterritorialize Mennonites with the idea that Mennonite values hold little promise for the present community, Reimer writes as if all Mennonite experience is both relevant and exciting for modern Mennonite Canadians. Not only does Reimer provide the new Mennonite community with a fiction that treasures its past experiences, he writes with an engaging style. His style announces his enjoyment of living: history, love, food, wine and tobacco, money making, the notorious, the banal. All human activities excite Reimer's imagination and find their way into his text.

Al Reimer is excessive in his style and, in that way, dangerous to major English. He exhibits no interest in or facility with moderate, restrained, careful lyrical prose. Instead, full of exuberance and love of Mennonite history, he provides more than enough information about more than enough topics all along the way. He is a bringer-in of the new for these reasons of his excessive, material style. English tends to mock his work because of its "long-windedness," but the book entertains all along the way, and if the reader were not as self-conscious about what she is to enjoy, this book, more than, say, David Bergen's intense presentations of the tangles of love couples, is like a wind in the hair, fresh and entertaining, full at every corner with a traditional Mennonite pleasure in the incontinent, the plentiful, the leisurely, the opulent, and so on. Preachers agonize, but also lust; stable boys fornicate and are caught; businessmen make much money; and so on. No high sentence against pleasure finds admittance in his works at all, full of the spirit of living as it is.

Suffering and pain in the lives of his characters do not suggest to Reimer that reterritorialization should occur at the level of alienation or despair. The novel's early passages describe with *élan* the arrival of the Mennonites in the region of the unhappy Cossacks.

> Grandfather Fast didn't know much more about the Nogaies except that one of their *auls*, or tent villages, had stood on the very spot selected as the site for Blumenau. When the Nogaies found that their fierce shouts and menacing gestures were ignored, they gave way sullenly to the big, stubborn *njemtsi*, the silent foreigners. Angrily, they struck their tents, loaded them onto huge oxcarts, and removed themselves from the accursed intruders. (12)

Here, historical details, foreign Russian language, Mennonite names for geographical places, and various other stylistic details moderate the implication of Mennonite selfishness. Even descriptions of suffering of a higher sort on many occasions during the course of the tale come to the reader with brandish, vitality, and verve. Whether he tells of drownings, break-ups of couples, lovers cheating, men drinking and killing, people beating each other up, and preachers meddling in individuals' businesses, he always finds each episode worthy of excitement and celebration. When, near the end of the novel, Reimer's narrator describes Nikolai's great weariness with a war he has helped wage, his style itself never reverts to weariness with life. Nikolai, in the savage Makhno's army as it pillages the Mennonite villages, wonders why everything must be destroyed. That is not how Mennonites as he knew them would do it.

> Mindless brutality disturbed him. And the destruction of property, the fine Mennonite *wirtschaften*. Why burn them? Why not save them for new owners? Destroying them was stupid, almost criminally wasteful. Anarchy didn't mean destroying everything in sight. It meant destroying the system and removing forcibly the people who had built the system and exploited it. (349)

Waste bothers even rebellious Nikolai, who reveres territorial traditions not a kopeck. He stands amid the ruins of his home place, imagining with florid sentimentality the philosophical purposes of destruction as the anarchists have theorized it.

> If only *Batko* [Makhno] could see it that way, but he
> believed destroying the human part of the system was not
> enough. Makhno argued, persuasively Nikolai had to admit,
> that you could only destroy *burzhuj* society by ruthlessly erad-
> icating everyone and everything in it. Hack it to pieces down
> to the very roots. Wipe out all physical traces. For him that
> was the only way. (349)

The imaginer of anarchy here pleads within himself, argues logic
internally, remembers what another thinks and speaks, names
things in a foreign tongue, and applies strong, vital verbs and
adverbs to the descriptions along the way. He aches but remains
interested. Nikolai's fulsome interior monologue suddenly turns its
attention to the images of the surrounding carnage.

> His thoughts were interrupted. The band was preparing to
> move out. He took a good look around. Many of the build-
> ings were still burning fiercely. Some had already crashed into
> fiery ruins. The smoke and heat and stench of burning was
> getting uncomfortable. The dead and wounded lay strewn
> around like abandoned sacks. The looting had been carried
> out with the usual messy greed and spilled waste. Food,
> clothing, items of furniture, lay about everywhere. The
> *tachankas* were heaped in teetering mounds. Someone had left
> a beautiful piano leaning crazily against a tree, abandoned at
> the last minute for want of room in the wagons. (349-50)

A terrible picture of destruction and waste, of Mennonite lives
and property mindlessly destroyed by the lowest common
denominator, vividly come home to the reader through the eyes
of one of the destroyers.

Despite the carnage, however, the pleasure of the text (with
the text's materiality and so its representation of the life force
itself) never leaves the narrator. He makes no artistic decision to
abandon life, even though history has apparently abandoned his
people. In the midst of even the most traumatic moments in
these pages, Nikolai the criminal finds it possible to imagine the
miraculous, much like Reimer's text stylistically declines to
employ a tone of alienation and opts for one much more
vigorous.

The terrified female screams had subsided to moans and pitiful gasps for help. Small children were wandering about sobbing, lost, and dazed. Nikolai had seen it all before, but felt himself stripped again to naked pity. And Uncle Hermann, was he able to get away? The farmstead where he was hiding was now also in flames, one of the last to go. (350)

And so, with miracle and suffering, end these particular pages that take us into the heart of Mennonite history in the place this people had to leave when they came to Canada. And in this lively materiality of his text, in imitation of the Mennonite belief and tradition that has always assumed the possibility of miracle in the midst of suffering, Reimer's style creates a new Mennonite group understanding. His artistic reterritorialization takes the best of the old and valiantly uses it—as a *bricoleur* would and does—to cobble together a picture of a vital future Mennonite community in the new world.

We have, then, two strongly contrasting methods of artistic reterritorialization in the prose of Bergen and Reimer. Each understands the need to represent the old in some way, and to imagine the new community Mennonites must form in order to remain a functioning group, one through the techniques of material restraint, the other through those of material excess. Each, in his own way, makes statements with his fiction about the possibilities and impossibilities of that far distant island that is the Mennonite community in the Canadian tempest.

2.

Army Surplus: Rudy Wiebe's
War and Peace and the Mennonite Church

Rudy Wiebe writes prolifically. Many of his works address the lives of Aboriginal Canadians: *The Temptations of Big Bear* (1973); *The Scorched Wood People* (1977); *A Discovery of Strangers* (1994); and, with Yvonne Johnson, *Stolen Life: The Journey of a Cree Woman* (1998). None, however, so directly addresses the relationship between Mennonites and Aboriginal Canadians as *Peace Shall Destroy Many* (1966).

Peace Shall Destroy Many is one of the first Mennonite novels, in either German or English, with a style recognizable and interesting to an English audience. The English readership expresses particular tastes, appetites, and expectations for literature. Still, Wiebe's novel resists replicating the common English novel, or a novel of the English Canadian centre, if there can be said to be such a centre. It is too political for that; it functions as a minor work of literature. Two questions need to be asked of this text and other minor texts. How is it political and so how does it carry community values? In what specific ways does it subvert major literature?

Minor literature announces itself by its inevitable political stance. Unlike major literature, it cannot keep its politics in the basement somewhere, in the narrative's "unconscious." Major literature, on the other hand, remains silent about itself because it assumes the obviousness of its politics, the universal knowledge of its values and social formations, and the needlessness of presenting for the reading public the conventions of its literature. Instead, major literature typically proceeds with a pure narrative unclouded by boring, didactic details. For major literature, a novel or book of poems must delight more than teach. Its assumptions and received wisdoms (the "teaching" part of a book) arrive courteously for the reader, already imbedded in the language itself, in the very ways that stories and even sentences unfold and construct themselves. Given this self-sufficiency of major literature, minor literature, by way of contrast, belongs much more with what major literature would call the silly and "Victorian" tendency of certain more religious works to attempt to teach their Christian gospel than with those works that provide a convincing plot and character development with these values quietly imbedded.

Contrary to the requirements of dominant literature in the twentieth century, Wiebe writes his novel for minor, non-major, didactic reasons. He wishes to inform Canadians of the true nature of Mennonite separateness and conscientious objection during the two world wars, and he wishes also to bring about an understanding within the Mennonite community itself of the ambiguities of its "simple" stand against violence. The Mennonite community needs the artist more than the preacher, Wiebe's novel implicitly but forcefully informs us, when it comes to understanding the complex reality of human life in the world. Explicitly, the novel argues that political and religious leaders, in their vulnerability to deceit, cloud our vision and simplify life's issues for private purposes and so fail as stewards of both knowledge and community values. Wiebe's novel attempts, in the manner of any minor work, to re-establish the community as a viable entity. The novel, representing the institution of art, strengthens what the other local institutions weaken. Art is stronger than the sword, more potent than church or state, in times of community crisis. Wiebe imagines only the success of art, however, and not the vulnerability of the artistic institution to degeneration. He remains unaware of the possibility that the artist might be a non-thinking leader in happy complicity with dominating technology.

The village of Wapiti is a young Mennonite village in the arable bushland of northern Saskatchewan. A dozen or so families live there and try to raise their families by traditional Mennonite ways and beliefs. The wise schoolteacher in the one-room country school falls into disrepute for his reformist views. The pretty, non-Mennonite woman who is also a schoolteacher causes a disturbance among the males of Wapiti, whose duty is supposed to be to hard work, not to pleasure and idleness. Apropos of such duty, certain ambitious and hard-working families in the community clash with another less industrious family that, true to the adage that equates cleanliness and godliness, has fallen from the strict adherence to Mennonite spiritual traditions connecting work and salvation. This renegade family, the Ungers, lives in the easy, natural lifestyle of their Métis neighbours, the Moosomins, rather than in that of their pious, church-going, capitalist brethren. Political issues also challenge the work ethic, as do those of work and household order. The war comes to Wapiti as a stirring of shame and nationalistic fervour in the breasts of its young males. Eventually, the struggle over the questions of the value of adherence to the faith of their fathers in the face of this dangerous patriotic call brings the novel to its climax with a physical confrontation of another sort right in the centre of the community.

The incidents of the story feature the interrelationships of three homesteading families, the Wienses, the Blocks, and the Ungers, with the indigenous Aboriginal Moosomin family. The year is 1944; the historical moment is the last part of World War II. The story's theme develops out of a collision between Mennonite belief in non-resistance, doctrinal conformity among its members, politico-religious separateness from the other people in the land, and Canadian nationalism during a period of war. The struggle certain young men from these families undergo in their confrontation with the local community's doctrine of non-resistance, prompted by both their consciousnesses and the animosity of Canadians whose family members have fought and died in this and the previous war, results in the disruption of various of the community's social formations. As events unfold, Wapiti experiences the decline of the hierarchical power structure by which the community has, till then, existed and thriven economically.

In brief, the plot involves the political protest of the sons of three adult members of the community, and one of its daughters. Thom Wiens is one of these, a diligent and obedient son, led by Joseph, an enlightened and thoughtful schoolteacher, to consider the problems inherent in conscientious objection. When Joseph eventually leaves Wapiti, coerced by local officials because of his non-conformist views, Elizabeth Block, shy, submissive to her father, the manipulative patriarch of Wapiti, quietly encourages Thom to also quit the Mennonite community, which she perceives as dangerous to his health. Pete Block, brother of Elizabeth and son of Peter Block, the said despot, faithfully obeys his father's teachings until an event involving the beautiful, single, female schoolteacher Miss Razia Tantamont brings him to a point of active resistance to community values. At this climactic point in the narrative, young Pete, in what we understand as a fit of jealous passion (though readers encounter a curious elision here concerning the specific motives for the struggle), challenges Hank Unger, the fighter ace, to a fist fight and knocks him down. Home on furlough, Hank has been too boldly eyeing Miss Tantamont and commenting on her former reputation in the army camps further east. Coming upon the two, Thom suddenly takes the courage of his convictions from those demonstrated by the actions of his friend Pete. In a nice confrontation between city and country, good and bad, profane and sacred, serious and sacrilegious, and lascivious and honourable, Thom knocks down Hank's brother Herb, who for years has publicly labelled him a coward, relentlessly mocking him for his refusal to fight either at home or on the front. Thom's and Pete's eleventh-hour display of resistance, or courage, whichever you wish to call it, breaks Deacon Block's indomitable will and leaves him alienated from the site of power in the community. Power relations have shifted in Wapiti at the end of the book, and the plot resists tying up this particular loose end. What will become of the community now with its views on obedience and pacifism assailed from within by its future leaders, and with its hierarchy of power publicly problematized?

To all intents and purposes, *Peace Shall Destroy Many* opens like any novel of pioneer life in rural Canada. The reader finds a little school, a teacher's bell clanging, students arriving for the day's classes from the four corners of the municipality, and even, of course, for pleasure's sake, for the sake of diversion from the seriousness of the novel (a seriousness not out of place in a canonical English novel), a couple of boys playing hooky.

> *The teacher stepped through the door and his bell clanged. When the distant measures of "O Canada" had faded over the tree-tips and the stirring flag on its pole was the only movement near the school, two overalled figures arose from behind a bush on the east hill and ran down its bare face.* (9)

These opening pages present the convention of the satirico-comical imbedded in the tragic to make an overall message more palatable. The two hooky-players bear the literary genes of Edgar in *King Lear,* Mr. Pumblechook in *Great Expectations,* and Tom Sawyer in *Huckleberry Finn.*

Peace Shall Destroy Many announces itself with this early light-heartedness as conventional, non-political, and English, but it is far from that. After the significantly brief, comical, two-page "Prelude," Chapter One immediately turns serious and political, a fact already foreshadowed by the information that the two vagrant boys are not only having fun but in their truancy resisting the values and laws of the community, an incipient though serious act of outlawhood: "The yellow planes passed overhead swiftly and in thunder" (11). The "yellow" invites; it speaks of the lure of the heroic and the warring. The sun-coloured planes promise in their power and brightness both swift death as well as a superiority of purpose, a "God on our side" omnipotence and beauty. Thom, like others in Wapiti, feels torn by these new signs of the technical and spiritual existence of a Canadian nation, signs that have been revealing themselves to this closed community for the last few years, ever since Canada joined the war effort. Boyish Thom succumbs to an attraction for the planes, to their power, to their speed, and to their charmed existence outside the monotony of farm life.

> Thom Wiens had heard their growing roar above the scrape of the plow on stones, but the trees hedged them from his sight.

Then suddenly, as he twisted on the halted plow to look back, they were over the poplars, flying low and fast. The sense of the horses' sweated trembling was in his rein-clenched hands as he stared the yellow planes out of sight to the north. (11)

Despite the lure of this power for him, Thom remains oblivious of his own ambivalence, made up of part longing for and part abjection at the thought of war. His rock-strong commitment to the Mennonite values never wavers:

> Fly, you heathen, he was thinking. Fly low, practise your dips and turns to terrify playing children and grandmothers gaunt in their rocking chairs. Practise your hawk-swoops, so you can gun down some equally godless German or bury a cowering family under the rubble of their home. To get paid for killing. To be trained to kill more efficiently. If you shoot down five Germans you get a medal. If you kill twenty at once, you get a Victoria Cross and the King himself shakes your hand. What will you do when all the Germans have been killed and the only work you know is shooting men? Acclaimed murderers everywhere! (11)

Regardless of his beliefs, more than a little envy and identification with the airplane pilots contaminate his thinking. Like many young men in times of war, Thom longs for the excitement of high military technology and for solidarity for a just cause, for the inner assurance that allows him to unequivocally claim goodness and rightness on his side while participating in the actions of saving his country. Such a language of good and right and saving, typically nationalist, implicit in Thom's struggle with his training, even sounds fully Mennonite. The fervour of Thom's beliefs in "Mennonitism" differs little in zealousness from any patriot's during wartime.

Thom notices none of these ambiguities, however, in his own passionate denunciation of the over-flying pilots. The planes fulfill the purpose of establishing the essential theme of *Peace Shall Destroy Many*, the novel's power as art. These symbols—the planes—effect here what symbols effect everywhere in the novel, a literary, symbolic reterritorialization of a weakened Wapiti community, a commitment of the community to be a community when the power of the leaders of its religious and political institutions no longer lead effectively. I will say more later of this symbolic (artistic) force for the strengthening of the community after an examination of the forces that weaken it.

I have mentioned Peter Block's controlling leadership of Wapiti. The novel presents the reasons for the community's extraordinary dependence on Block as a conflict between traditional beliefs and the new challenges that the Canadian soil and society force these traditions to face. When all other Wapiti Mennonites are left uncertain in the face of the new land's deterritorializing forces, Block remains steadfastly and absolutely certain of the rules and codes to adhere to. He leads and governs his fearful people by himself refusing to show fear or doubt. Three incidents—the yellow planes flying overhead, the happiness of Thom Wiens's brother Hal contrasted to his own discontent, and a lengthy mimetic section concerning the specific moral dependence of the Wienses on Peter Block—early on establish the nature of Thom's, and the community's, dilemma. We have seen how Thom simultaneously is moved by and condemns the flying planes (they fly above him not like some dark force or some evil hated thing, but "swiftly and in thunder," so he chooses a positive description of what in the logic of his speech he criticizes).

> To grow something took a long time, and the machines for it were slow. There were no machines to pick rocks. But the machines for death were wind-swift. For a moment he felt he had discovered a great truth, veiled until now: the long growing of life and the quick irrevocableness of death. (12)

The farm boy would like to have machines reduce the hard labour of breaking soil, but he knows that machinery also causes destruction and so is suspect. The need to love and distrust simultaneously characterizes Thom's as well as Mennonite life generally. For the territorial Mennonite, always in everything an imperative exists commanding his truthfulness and honesty. He must uncover truth somehow, sometimes by honest searching, sometimes by deceit, but primarily by paying it lip service. In Thom's case (in contrast to that of many others in the novel), lip-service honesty hardly applies. He legitimately searches. Yet the search confuses him. Confusion over truth, in fact, features foremost in Thom's character. He wishes to accept the teachings of his father and the church regarding truth but he worries over the credibility of these teachings and feels torn two ways in consequence.

His inherited patriarchal (religious and political) values appear clear to him. He knows them by heart. He longs to fulfill what they require of him, what they require of the group subject.

> The heaped rocks recalled him, and he turned to stride rapidly towards the plow. To just stand, thinking! He glanced about, happy for the rugged world that had hidden his dreaming. Pulling his feet up hard with each step, he sensed within himself the strength of his forefathers who had plowed and subdued the earth before him. He, like them, was working out God's promise that man would eat his bread in the sweat of his face, not pushing a button to watch a divine creation blaze to earth. (12)

Hard work allows him and others of his community to forge ahead without thinking. Thom's training tells him the propriety and goodness of resignation to previous thinking and acceptance of received wisdom. "You don't need to think about the meaning of 'in the sweat of his brow' since that thinking has been already done by the Holy Bible and a few unknown ancestors who did *that* hard work for you," tradition teaches. Still, something in his experience of the moment bothers him and forces him to doubt, if only momentarily, the rules to which, after such doubts, he immediately recommits himself.

Such unchallenged acceptance of rules hardly equips Thom and his fellows for relations in this new land. Preacher Goertzen teaches, for instance, that Mennonites both know more than others in the world because of "God's Grace" (12), and that what they know, of which others remain ignorant, truly defines the meaning of love.

> "We are to follow Christ's steps, but we do not have pride. By God's Grace we understand what others do not. As we cannot imagine Him lifting a hand to defend himself physically, so we, His followers, conquer only by spiritual love and not by physical force. Always only love: for those who love us, for those indifferent to us, for those who hate us, for those who would kill us, which is the same thing; *all* are included when

He says, 'This is my commandment, that you love one another even as I have loved you.'" (12)

We know the truth of love, Goertzen says, and our actions must
never compromise that knowledge of love's nature. Obedience to
labour, in suffering, against a resistant earth constitutes the first
lesson a Mennonite learns, then, and the prescription, for
Christ's sake, to love others, the second. Of course, such love
means to not kill others in war, as Thom earlier informs readers.

Herein, in this double restriction, lies the problem for Thom,
a problem that takes him the entire narrative to understand, to
face and then to act to resolve. He wishes to believe, but finds
himself immediately driven to doubt (as the passages which follow show directly and indirectly). This bifurcation holds for the
question of work as surely as for that of love raised by Goertzen.
Labour is fine, Thom acknowledges, and the earth is the enemy
he admits, but his construction of rightness differs from the sensations he feels when close to the earth. His beliefs and feelings
oppose each other. "Thom felt the ground warming with expectation, the ripeness of the earth's belly pushing itself up against
the steel of the shares" (13). Biblically prescribed labour "properly" tears at the enemy earth, with "steel" shares, which rip at the
"ripeness of the earth's belly." The earth, in the narrator's imagination, cooperates in human exertions against her. Yet, the shares
are the enemy, the perpetrators of violence against a gentle, giving, though somewhat masochistic, earth.

Peace Shall Destroy Many presents the earth as if the fault lies
with her somehow that men toil on her. She affects him as
duplicitous, as both seductive, gentle, procreative, a woman,
but also as requiring of him control and violence to constrain
her exuberance and keep her seductive charm at bay. Wiebe
gives us in Thom the essential Mennonite farming youth
indoctrinated with visions of the corrupt earth, which deserves
what it gets from the aspiring human spirit, a classical concep-
tion equal to anything in Milton or even Plato. Christian tradition, of course, teaches that our "Edenic" existence deceives
us. It seduces and charms in order to lure us to spiritual death.
We must not submit to its siren beauty and call. Thom indicates the character of his eventual resistance to Mennonite

dualistic doctrine early on here. Even when he later rebels against this classical, authoritative, humanistic model of earth's relation to heaven, he still remains uncommitted to a new view that reveres the earth, willing to fight only for the shallow purpose of protecting property.

The text brims with the contradiction between old-world belief and new-world place. In the passage above, as elsewhere, Thom cannot get past his forefathers' teachings and fails to understand the earth. The earth coaxes humans from inordinate labour, as Herb Unger discovers in his preference for pleasuring in the meadows over suffering behind the plough (76 ff), and as the Aboriginal man Two Poles and the Métis Moosomins perennially know in their slow and patient ways. Thom senses, without defining it as such, duplicity in everything. To love the earth might not mean to labour in and against it. Thom's body understands love for the earth better than his head.

> When he lay with his face in the sandy loam, arms and legs yearning, he was beyond himself. It seemed to Thom that every man must feel the smallness and the greatness, his face in the dirt when the clouds were sheep with their heads down in the sunshine of the open sky and the larks chanting from their post-perch and the burdened horses nodding their heads to earth with sweat black in straggles down their thighs. Lying there, he felt doubts settle in his mind like mud in the hollows of the spring-soaked land. (13)

This image of "yearning" for earth, and being transported "beyond himself" derives from a generative view of the earth. Good bottom land depends on the accumulation of alluvial soil. Here things can grow. Rich soil forms the land in a slow, peaceful becoming. Growth needs such slow, peaceful accretion.

But the pastoral image above also tells of destruction. In the midst of his reverie about larks, horses and settling mud, Thom characteristically recalls human hatred, harboured more by foreigners than Canadians. "The earth holding him, he thought, if only there were enough trees and hills and rocks in all Saskatchewan or all Canada or even all the world to hide us from a Hitler who has tasted power like a boar's first gulp of warm blood" (13). "We are good, they are bad," Thom implies, much like his knowledge tells him that the earth corrupts and work perfects. Precisely in such self-congratulatory assumptions, however, Mennonite consciousness remains inadequate to deal with the new place of their recent occupation. The Mennonite love of the physical is always kept subordinate to the need to subordinate the love for the physical and so Thom and the other members of the Mennonite community are stuck landless, without a rootedness in the land to which they have moved. The novel, writing the physicality of Mennonite life, writing its spiritual tyranny, and writing its fears and hopes, brings about the possibility of the Mennonite community becoming part of the land that adopts them. The novel's art gives the Mennonites a sensual, corporal territory here, which they prefer to defer to the non-territory of some transcendent world. Material, here and now, of this world, the novel's art reterritorializes (gives a functional body of codes and rules to) a dysfunctional Mennonite community.

Self-congratulation inadequately substitutes for understanding, Thom gradually learns in the course of the narrative, because it presumes to differentiate the worthy from the unworthy. It makes treacherous assumptions that the false and the true exist. Had Mennonites left their beliefs at home when they came over to this land, they would have been better equipped to deal with local realities, which they violently misunderstand. Not knowing the danger of belief systems to all that is in the new land when they come, not knowing about respect, courtesy and neighbourliness (since these values must never, the group knows, supercede piety, fervency, and the outward show of being good and loving), not willing, of course, to abandon their till then hard-earned faith and beliefs, they damage beyond telling their new home and its indigenous inhabitants. In other words, their belief systems, which call for neighbourliness, require Mennonites when they arrive here to practise the very opposite of neighbourliness toward those indigenous to the land. Somehow the belief system of Mennonites allows them to put the survival of the group first before the practice of kindness to neighbours. What had been developed in Russia as a way of dealing with place and people no longer holds here in Canada with equal effect. In fact, the Mennonite Russian ways falter here, especially as prescribed by law and regulation and not produced by group experience or the subject's individual construction.

Mennonite belief imported from Europe and Russia turns a blind eye to the worth of the indigenous Canadians who, for the most part, benignly share their land with these newcomers. Tyrants and terrorists, the newcomers grab for themselves whatever they see and walk on. Wiebe's Mennonites think of Aboriginal people as loafers who just aimlessly spend their time in, and not at work on, the forests and grasslands. Block and the citizens of Wapiti believe that all shiftless people must be "bought out" and moved off the valuable land. "If it's not productive (in the capitalist sense of overproduction), it's not being properly husbanded," a Mennonite truism goes even today.

Unable to imagine the Aboriginal people as fellow subjects, as fellow humans, the inhabitants of Wapiti, including Thom, speak of them as a nuisance to be adroitly expressed from their holdings:

> . . . but to the highway on the east, Poplar Lake on the west, and to the Indian reservation across the Wapiti River to the north, all around the Mennonite settlement lay virgin sections, heavily wooded, enough for children's children. And there would be more, when the last breeds were bought out. (20-21)

Heavily coded biblically, this passage combines the essential literary, symbolic elements that enrich western literature: sex, family, the aesthetic imagination, place, and ethnic specificity. We get sex in "virginity" (with its ironic, duplicitous understanding, and alacritous artistic relevance to the density of the novel, of "virgin." "Virgin" reflects the sex that Mennonites fear so deeply, from which they anxiously work to escape, which they wrestle to control in the land, which they destroy by trying to master, and about and against which they teach and preach incessantly). We get in this passage also "the heavy woods" of the rich German imagination. We find, furthermore, a particular group of Wapiti ethnic Mennonites in a particular location in central Canada. We see the Abrahamic family in "children's children" (with its overdeterminining valuing, in the original Hebraic story, of colonialization and procurement by divine promise of land and wealth, and a reason for the sustaining of a war mentality to protect all these classical markers of a nation's wealth). Wiebe heavily codes this passage, then, with literary symbolism and allusiveness.

More important than and yet part of its presentation of Western literary symbols, however, the passage establishes how poorly Mennonites think (as all minor groups, all groups, really, have trouble thinking their blindness and their privilege) about the connections between the Bible's truths and the translation of these truths into action in the new land. Thom acts as no exception, as confused and unable to think these connections as anyone else. Paradoxically, the novel helps the reader—in part by showing Thom's confused thinking at work—to think through the vicious irony of preaching love and non-resistance while simultaneously coercing the Aboriginal people off their traditional lands. Aboriginal territory in Canada had its own complex system of sustaining rules and codes. Mennonites contributed to their deterritorialization. Without the novel, however, without the aid of art, the major (in this case, the Mennonite community under consideration) mistakes its untruth for truth and this artistic wisdom is the heartbeat of Wiebe's accomplishment. Without itself fully understanding this problem of Mennonites disrespecting the Aboriginal Canadians whose land they systematically steal, the novel challenges the poor thinking tolerated by Mennonites in their argument for peace in their communities, for non-resistance in each country to which they wander.

Thom resists Block's tyranny in the end, but even then he does not properly understand the way that the entire lifestyle in which the Mennonites have been engaged in the new land is a violent and aggressive one, an appropriation from the people who were kind to them and whom they force from their homeland. Their violence against the territory of Aboriginal people is as indifferent to human suffering as that which forces people in Poland, Germany, and Austria from their homelands in the particular war this novel constructs for its readers. In other words, the same people who through active non-resistance resist the ills of war, one of which is the unfair dispossession of people from their territory, are blind to their own equally callous uprooting of and alienation of Aboriginal people from traditional territories.

Block functions, as we see above and as evidence below will

show, as a despot. He presides over and promotes a despotic religion and politics. An authority figure, he reminds Wapiti Mennonites of their heritage. Human products of the new land, Joseph, Thom, and young Peter, actively resist Block's authority, reluctantly at first, and finally with full conviction. They show the community by their questioning and ultimately by their actions the narrowness and inadequacy of its outmoded thinking. They point to the need for new values. Thom feels early on in the novel that the wrong values control the voices of the group. Joseph's treatment at the hands of church leaders initiates some of Thom's earliest doubts. Questioned about his reasons for teaching Sunday School in English at a local picnic, a first-time occurrence for such a travesty in the memory of the German-speaking communities, the elders coldly judge Joseph and excommunicate him from the church. Thom reflects on the community's vacant values.

> There was a rustle as Joseph arose for the last time. Beyond his own numbed incapacity, there welled in Thom the overwhelming feeling that something of immense value was being abused here. As if Joseph's beliefs were being used to coerce him into the virtue of asking forgiveness where there was nothing to forgive. Only two, from the back benches, had supported the teacher; there was no further sound now. (62)

The very stature of the judging "brotherhood" (church elders) and their physical attitude in the church as Joseph waits to reply tells the story of their deceit and impassivity. If he begs forgiveness, he remains a member in good standing. So vital is the lie to the solidarity of this group, and likely to that of all large groups. Only in the complicity of lies and secrecy accepted as truth may the group persist as a group without change.

> Thom could see before him, erect and half-turned to Joseph, waiting: Rempel's face ham-like, Block's sharp and clean as a knife, Reimer's gleaming head, Pa hopeful, pen poised; the younger men, Ernst, young Franz, Pete, the Rempel twins beyond, had their eyes hard on their shoes. (62)

But where will such reformation, as that begun by Thom, Pete, and Joseph, halt? Does it mean the disintegration of the community? The answer lies in the description of the conflict itself, in the self-analysis that puts the problem up to the light for public inspection, including the problem of the reforming impulse itself. In other words, the novel as a work, introspective, somewhat objective and impartial, analyzing the conflict between the community's values and the deterritorializing forces in the world that assail these values, the novel that writes the story of this struggle against traditions, creates new community spirit.

Art as an institution brings together the people whom religion and political action had discouraged and left feeling bereft of purpose and cohesion, bereft, that is, of a sense of group unity. Minor art reterritorializes a community when the religious and political institutions have destroyed it. Block, with his greediness, cowardice, thoughtlessness, and inadequate dispositions exposed by the protagonist of this novel, bows his head, led away by those he once led (these qualities of Block become clear in the argument which follows).

> The Deacon bowed his scarred grey head to his hands, and the men of Wapiti community, Métis and Mennonite, standing in an old barn, heard the sobs of a great strong man, suddenly bereft, and broken. They heard, terrified . . . Block had been led away by Pastor Lepp, with Pete following silently. (236-37)

Thom, announcing to all the nature of his uncertainties, the fragility of his politics, assumes that his enemy's secrets only *appear* formidable and confronts him openly. Thom exposes himself to public scrutiny at this moment for the first time, at this moment when, after a lifetime of wishing to confront a leader who controls but controls without thinking, without graciousness, and without care for others, he fights his old enemy and knocks him down. This act of public violence within the community, in contrast to Block's frequent secret acts of violence, is the moment of Thom's open confrontation of Deacon Block. It is the announcing of the failure of Wapiti's political leadership to guide and lead the community.

True, he already shows signs of wishing to make himself vulnerable in, for instance, the scene with Block when he takes the courage to ask him about Sunday School teaching and about the death of Elizabeth ("Elizabeth told me herself that day . . ." 208). Thom practises such an "honest" self-analysis again when he admits that the brotherhood's position against Joseph deceives the community and indulges its fear of change and thought: "As the deep voices about him echoed 'Amen,' his mind could only dully comprehend that in all the talking that evening, no one had disposed of any of Joseph's questions. They had not even been considered" (63). After a series of failures at vulnerability, Thom eventually stands up to the enemy, to secrecy hiding a fear of change and of exposure. Thom, fighting his enemy, refuses to be determined by the Mennonite theocratic state and ushers in, with this refusal, the possibility of a new, revitalized Mennonite group, which will now consist of those who still cling to the old ways and precepts, as well as of those who, like himself, find the energy to move toward a new state in the future based on this act of courage and self-exposure.

Thom, though bitten with uneasiness at the special privilege Block enjoys, initially considers him a man of great wisdom, deserving special respect. Thom's father reflects on Block's importance for Wapiti: "For Wiens, as for his third son, there was one rock in the whirlpool of the Canadian world. They were both thinking of him at the same time. Deacon Peter Block" (21). Block enjoys, thus, because of such deferential treatment, "respect capital" and "linguistic capital" as well as more traditional forms of capital. He advises and governs by a language familiar to himself, a language only partially available to others. He enjoys privileged economic capital; his farm flourishes partly as a result of the willingness of others to support him in hard times because they owed him allegiance from the early days of the community in Canada, when he helped various poor settlers establish their homesteads. He enjoys privileged capital, as the reader gradually discovers, despite his personal, secret history of wicked, violent actions in a community that officially deplores wickedness and violence.

Wiebe provides various examples of Block's violence in both Russia and Canada. In Russia, he secretly hoarded food, and, as a consequence, caused the starvation death of at least one poor family there. Furthermore, some time before their emigration, in a fit of rage, he beat a Cossack peasant to death, ironically in a pathetic, self-righteous argument over the impoverished Cossack's hiding of food. In Canada later, to add to the list, he decides to kill Louis Moosomin, the lover of Elizabeth and father of her unborn child. He furthermore spearheads the ruthless dispossession of Aboriginal people from their land in the vicinity of Wapiti in order to make more room for the new Mennonite settlers. The major assumes privileges for itself because it believes itself more deserving than others, not naturally, but because of a willing adherence to certain morals and beliefs. It sees the Aboriginal indifference to particular beliefs as a sign of godlessness and therefore as something to be wiped out, as if "God" would not care for subjects of his who neglected to live by the virtues established by Mennonite codes. These codes, conveniently for Mennonites here on earth, as the belief goes, are codes established in heaven and available to anyone with the will, energy, stick-to-it-iveness, and industry to adopt as his own. Privilege, my logic suggests, derives inevitably from belief.

Peace Shall Destroy Many helps us think about Mennonites, the minor status of Mennonite art. Block, both religious and political leader of Wapiti, has arrived at the place in his long control of the thought and action of the group he has subjected, in both senses of the word (oppressed and constructed according to his understanding of the Bible and his own despotic agenda), where his tenure and leadership are about to be challenged and successfully opposed by others in Wapiti besides Thom. That is in the novel's future, however, and constitutes its main narrative thrust. For now it is enough to say that this novel, standing for a third institution, that of art, attempts through intense symbolism to bring about a reterritorialization of community that religion and politics are on the verge of destroying, if it is not exactly destruction they cause. They cause a deterritorialization of the cohesive group by pointing out the outmodedness, harshness, sterility, and unreliability of their laws and regulations. Now the time has come to inspire the failing community with another and very powerful social structure, as I have said. The novel has the potential to hold up to the minor community new avenues for escape from the destruction they witness around them in the guise of broken religious laws and inept political practices.

Thom, coming after Joseph in questioning the community's understanding of the biblical call to pacifism, contributes to the razing of the ineffectual politico-religious institutions as Wiebe contributes to a new vision for the community, based on questioning the old regulations and beliefs. In this novel, with its narrative of struggle and final victory, Wiebe says to all Mennonite readers, "Listen to my story. You all have a problem, which needs addressing. The community is being destroyed by the deceitfulness of your religious leaders, by the Peter Blocks in your villages, and the question of our Mennonite responsibility to the outer and larger community must be not only addressed, but presented as a serious and important issue."

3.

Laughering at Ourselves:
Armin Wiebe and the Mennonite Appetite

Armin Wiebe's three novels (*The Salvation of Yasch Siemens*, 1984, *Murder in Gutenthal*, 1991 and *The Second Coming of Yeeat Shpanst*, 1995, all Turnstone Press) celebrate Mennonite material culture, though none as robustly as *The Salvation of Yasch Siemens*. I choose Armin Wiebe for the subject of the third chapter because his material, strongly minor style in the first two-thirds of *Salvation*, helps me to explain and define material literature. This explanation of the material literary method in turn sets up the examination to follow of the material and lyrical poetics of Patrick Friesen and Di Brandt.

An analyst of Armin Wiebe's first novel might well conclude that Wiebe's narrative strategies in the end spiritualize what has begun as a material text about a material community of Mennonite Canadians. This self-resistance is an important quality of the novel, but Wiebe's real achievement is his presentation of the Mennonite community in its "reality"; that is, in its corporeality: its flows and motions and differences, myriad and unrecordable in their entirety.

Yasch Siemens, a poor "orphan" boy, pulls himself up by his bootstraps through relentless industry, elbow grease, ingenuity, and an indomitable drive to succeed. A classic rags-to-riches story, the novel has Yasch growing up in the village of Gutenthal with his *muttachi*, as doughty and salt-of-the-earth a backwoods farming mother as you might find anywhere. Yasch's father long since "went dead" in Mexico to where he "clawed out" (*ootjekleift*—escaped). He dies of a knife in the back from a jealous husband/lover of the "Spanish" girl he drives around in his convertible over there. His mother tells him this version of his father's story, but Yasch feels uninformed in his attempt to piece together the man's real life and character. This subplot—his mother's accounts of his father, and Yasch's uncertainty about her tales—makes Wiebe's story an archetypal "quest for the father" novel. Yasch, who himself is married at the time, questions his mother's requirement that he share in the "women's work." He hopes that she will stand by his intent not to wash dishes at home, a chore he believes his wife Oata should handle.

> I try to reckon out when I ever saw my Futtachi wash dishes or cook something and I'm thinking through when I was young and the things I can remember about my dad and all I can remember is about the time me and him cut pigs together. (156)

He "gribbles" (*grebble*—puzzle) at length about his father's sharing kitchen work. The sudden realization of its exact place and time comes to him connected with the tragic absence of other siblings in the family.

> . . . and that was when Futtachi washed dishes. He didn't leave them for Muttachi to do when she got home. Even a few days later when Muttachi came home and there was no baby along and Futtachi said the hospital didn't have one fixed ready for us and Muttachi just went to bed and she stayed in bed for a long time, Futtachi was almost all the time cooking and washing dishes and I can't remember that he ever complained that he had to do women's work. (157)

The old man could do household chores and so can Yasch, the protagonist decides. "What was good for him is good for me." And so the quest for the father ends, with the son learning to respect and love the female world because the previous generation did the work of imagining such "unnatural" respect for him.

With a sigh, he continues now on his own way, unencumbered by worries and concerns of such a higher sort. High philosophical concerns (feminism and its various questions about the intrinsic value of women) at this point recede in the distance, properly dealt with and incorporated by the protagonist, whose sons now will have to arrive at similar, difficult though rewarding, discoveries about their father in good time.

Though at times major in its themes and conventions, as in this quest-for-the-father motif, much more importantly as a minor text *The Salvation of Yasch Siemens* zooms in on the Mennonite "interior." The novel presents with affect the antics and desires of the irrepressible, quintessentially Low German Mennonite, Yasch Siemens. Yasch's narrative life divides itself into episodes around his three loves—two great loves for Fleeda Schreeda and for Sadie Nickel, and one love of convenience for fat Oata, which turns into what readers of realism would be tempted to call his "true love," spiritual in its physicality. The Puritanism in literary realism is obvious. To all intents and purposes, Armin Wiebe *teaches* us something, preaching to us at the novel's close. His purpose seems to be to tell us that the conservative, the moderate, the plain, and the hard working—in other words desire as lack, Oata instead of Sadie for lover and wife—offer a secret reward of great value and an ability to satisfy in the end if only the individual shows stick-to-itiveness, keeps a stiff upper lip, and learns responsibility. Anglican-Protestant rhetoric, and Mennonite discourse. Learn to sacrifice here on earth, and all these things shall be added unto thee.

The Salvation of Yasch Siemens tells the story of a poor Mennonite farm boy who makes good. Yasch Siemens grows up with one parent, his mother only, because his father has been murdered in "Mennonite" Mexico over a Spanish woman. The stigma of his father's scandalous death and of his landless status—having no farm of his own nor farming machinery, scratching out a living with the often contemptuous charity and long-suffering of wealthy neighbours and of the church—fill Yasch with an unusual industry and a will to succeed. He is clever, opportunistic, scrappy, and hungrier for success at whatever cost than most of his fellows. Though he speaks conventional Mennonite morality, though he brims with aphorisms and oral wisdoms about decency, honesty, and kindness, his interest lies mainly in his own promotion. This self-promotion characterizes him at least until near the very end of the novel, when children are born to him and Oata, a propertied farmer's daughter whom he marries for the half-section she brings as dowry. The children's presence (though not their actions or subjective characters) somehow mellows Yasch. Their presence teaches him empathy. Love for mankind seems to have come attached to the children like a covering letter.

> Sure, Yasch Siemens isn't a bigshot farmer like the others, but it's not so bad really. With only a half-section I can really farm it, and I don't think I have any more wild oats and mustard than the neighbours who use all that Avadex BW and Hoe-grass stuff they show sliding on a curling rink on TV. In the winter time I read things about organic farming and I don't know but for a small outfit like mine it seems to work. A farmer always has worries but it sure doesn't seem so bad when you don't have to worry about feeding the bank manager's family, the lawyer's family and the implement dealer's family. But then Oata helps, too. She makes a big garden and we have our own chickens, pigs, cows and things so we hardly even have to worry about feeding the storeman's family yet, too. Doft sometimes wants to know how come he can't have one of those games that you play with the TV like the neighbours' boys have but I just laugh and say that while those guys are playing with themselves on TV he can play with their girlfriends. (165)

Besides the surprise of new competence in love, this passage reveals a great deal about *Salvation*'s thematic method. First of all, it shows us Yasch's growth in practicality and wisdom. The stork brings wisdom in its satchel and Yasch suddenly sees the real value of the small family farm instead of the "bigshot" one. He displays an ecological smartness, resisting now the use of unnecessary farming chemicals on his land, a self-righteousness that running a small operation makes possible. He not only recognizes the average worker's debt to the big corporations, to banks, the justice system, and the business institution, but contrives how to avoid contributing to their upkeep by using organic methods, a heroic wisdom that almost no farmer ever grasps, certainly no one else in Gutenthal, regardless of wealth or status.

In addition to all this new wisdom, Yasch even commendably feels growing convictions about the rights of women, a wisdom of special merit. It would seem from what precedes in the narrative, as well as from the subject matter of other Mennonite Canadian literature that *Salvation* necessarily reflects, that males remain virtually ignorant of female rights in "redneck" and patriarchal, rural Mennonite country. In this backward land, political feminist discourse teaches, wives and daughters performed and still perform most of the actual farm labour while their grudging, pampered, self-satisfied husbands, fathers, and sons lay down the law and drive around in pickup trucks and tractors, an unfair division of labour upheld by and preached from the pulpit. Oata, a male-feminist Yasch prudently comes to realize, contributes a great deal to the Needarp farm's independence from the grasping service institutions by keeping a garden and raising chickens and livestock.

Furthermore, our fast-maturing hero handles *the* most difficult feat of the late twentieth century in the Western world simply and adroitly: he parents superbly. Because of Yasch's timely wisdom, instead of staying neurotic and masturbatory like the other young boys of Gutenthal, Doft promises to grow up generative, "play[ing] with their girlfriends" instead of with TV games (games and thematic narcissism foreshadowed in the first chapter by the TV tower episode in which young Yasch "plays" with the younger of the Schroeder sisters while on a treacherous "heroic" ascent and descent, not into and out of hell, but into the sky via the TV tower on the American side of the border close to Gutenthal). This passage about Doft playing with the other boys' girlfriends shows Yasch parenting with wisdom and with a winning panache. How appropriate for Doft (the novel makes no mention of the daughter and her sexuality) to outwit and outdo the poorly parented, overindulged neighbourhood boys by playing well the real game of sex, while they glue their foolish attentions to television games (technology, the corporations, the banks and lawyers and businesses).

In other words, Doft wins over the other boys at a host of activities that their fathers alone could teach them to win at, provided they behaved with Yasch's diligence and worldly wisdom: how to be independent of the horde of other boys, how to enjoy sex despite the strict Mennonite mores against it and prove thereby their own enlightenment and possibilities for joy and freedom from endless Mennonite morality; how to rebel and get away with it; how to create community (play with others) instead of atrophying socially "playing with yourself"; and how to grow up healthy with their biological desires sated. In a final bit of wisdom, Yasch says here, *his* boy will not have to grow up fatherless, debilitated by setbacks the orphan faces growing up alone in the treacherous economic world. This father will be there to advise, to strategize, to provide cash and material needs, and most of all to contribute through his own serious experiences of impecuniousness to the balance of the thought and action of his children.

Unlike on other occasions, Yasch does not "laugher" himself on the topic of his children at this late "mature" stage in his life. He simply does the proper "major" thing one does to make a solemn point that transcends the minor play with language in which the rest of the minor text is set: he "laughs" (165) in perfect capital E English at his boy's foolish, unwise desires and shows him a better way, pointing him cleverly, considering the capitalist theme of the text, away from technological possessions to ones that do not cost, and which both gratify more and at the same time subvert Mennonite Canadian anti-sexual morality. At a few critical points in this otherwise minor English novel, which deterritorializes major English through steady mistranslation of English meaning by supplying a laughable and outrageous coinage (such as the constant "what is loose" standing for "what is wrong," which derives from the low German *vaut ess louse*, meaning precisely in Low German "what is loose" but not meaning that, or not meaning much of anything, in context in English; except, of course, that whenever something is wrong, there is a powerful sense of the looseness of what gives meaning in the world, the looseness of the individual subject's connections with the group, the looseness of the connections between things, ideas, and meanings, which before made perfect sense and seemed more tightly connected).

Yes, Yasch Siemens parents well. He is here, at the end of the novel, the wise father. Where his father failed, Yasch succeeds. But all this success, this newly successful Yasch, an exemplum suddenly of spiritual values rooted in religious permanence and showing the rewards of persistence and self-sacrifice, comes late in the novel. Before this, in the more authentically minor and deterritorialized (and so more communal and social) first nine chapters of the novel, Wiebe draws a more profound picture of the material Mennonite subject who hides his materiality from himself and others.

In his confession in Chapter Eight, Yasch tells of atrocities committed on his person and a few other innocent schoolfellows many years ago by Forscha Friesen ("Bullying and Pushy" Friesen). Forscha Friesen, now sitting smugly in church, listening to Yasch's confession, once made organized games in school impossible. He rode his team of make-believe horses around the schoolyard, breaking up attempts at baseball and other games. Always mean and destructive as a child, now an upstanding member of the church with too much influence, he directs with disquieting power the goings-on of various church functions, including the "Christian Endeavor Evening." For one of these evenings, in fact, Forscha spitefully selects Yasch to give a testimony. A testimony is a public and highly ritualistic, conventional profession of faith in which you tell your "faith story": the moment of personal commitment to Christ; how you have both succeeded and failed in your previous relationship with Him; and especially where you have "backslidden" and "strayed from the path." No young person deliberately confesses in public. Forscha's wicked intent for revenge on Yasch for Yasch's refusal to join his gang of disrupters on the school ground years earlier directs him to select Yasch for a testimony candidate. He knows it will "nerk" ("spite" and "taunt") him into blackening his name further in the community.

> This going to church business just makes me feel more cut off. And then to have to deal with Forscha Friesen yet. I see him standing there so shtollt and Christlich while the last prayer is prayed and when he thinks nobody is looking he turns his head and he looks me on with those light green eyes with dark centres and I can see that for sure he is the same Forscha that used to be boss of the school yard and that this testimony thing is his way to nerk me. (123)

But once selected, Yasch may decline giving the testimony only at great cost to himself.

The "Confession Scene" begins with Yasch's recollection of the scene as it unfolded earlier. One cannot always be hypocritical even if one wants to, Yasch says. He labours to be both honest and hypocritical about his sinful past so the church will accept him because of the effort of humility.

> So simple it isn't. Sure, I have hauled a few twenty-fours out from the parlor and before I go dead there's lots of chance that I will haul out some more. But I can affirm on a stack of Bibles that I never even sniffed a bottle cap that day. If I had, for sure I would have stayed home from church and people would say, "That Yasch Siemens sure is a dow-nix!" like always they have and they could have felt shtollt and fromm about it and it would still hail the same on the good man's field as on the bad man's and the rooster would still crow in the morning. And nobody would think that in the Gutenthal church the Devil had been. (117)

Shtollt means "proud," and *fromm* means "pious and religious." If he had not made his confession, Yasch says, people could have gone along blindly as they did before, believing themselves superior, by God's design, to himself and others such as he. Now, however, the eyes of complacent people have been opened, they have been forced to see "reality" in a light they did not want to see it in, and they make the ambiguous assessment, Yasch claims, of having a church now contaminated by the very presence of the Devil. Who exactly, this ambiguity asks us to consider, is this Devil: Yasch or the men and women at whom Yasch points the finger? In this context, in other words, the true confession is the false confession.

Yasch gives a true confession, which is not believed by his fellow church members. And yet, why confess at all? If a Mennonite shuns confession, once perceived as living outside the moral standards set by "God" and the church, he cannot properly belong in the community. He experiences limited access to financial institutions (as Yasch's thwarted efforts to buy Yut Yut Leeven's land on credit shows); he suddenly lacks friends to phone, to ask for help, or from whom to borrow machinery when his breaks down; he finds himself without cozy commercial contacts for discounts on machinery. Subversive and independent, the outspoken group subject stands alone and lonely in such a community. If he intends to succeed, he must accept the code of the communal hypocritical standards *as if they were honesty*. Yasch makes a bad confession. He fails to accomplish in his confession what a confession should accomplish, humbling himself as the confessing subject before his judges, the members of the church (subjected group), declaring his sinfulness (his cavalier treatment and subversion of their rules and regulations), and with a contrite heart and because of a contrite heart, finding acceptance back into the fold of the group from which his sin (rebellion) now excludes him.

Yasch claims honest initial intentions, though he only reluctantly attends the church meeting in the end, going because Oata insists: "Some things an honest man can't lie about. I mean, I tried. For Oata I really tried" (117). He feels a great discomfort as the moment arrives to open up his private world to the general public.

> Oata gives me one with her elbow and she fuschels in my ear that it is time for the testimony, so I grip my Bible on tight and stand up and start to walk to the front and then all of a sudden I am climbing the steps up to the platform and I am almost to the pulpit when I see the preacher that is supposed to talk after I give the testimony. . . . (142)

The long description of the approach heightens the tension of this feared moment of self-exposure and self-surveillance. The distance to the front seems far. When he steps up to the pulpit, however, an unexpected emotion fills him.

> I step behind the pulpit and put my Bible down on the slanted thing there and I reach my hand out for the nickel-colored microphone that looks like the front from a Massey Harris 44 and I move it so that I can talk it in without bending over too much, just like the preachers do. Then I look at the church. (143)

The critical moment has passed. The hardware up on stage already gives him a lift. The microphone reminds him comfortably of farming equipment, of a *powerful* farm tractor. He instinctively manoeuvres the microphone to let him speak with dignity and style, not bent over the way a less self-possessed young person might. This little act reveals the showman in Yasch. This public speaking might not be so bad after all. It might be, in fact, just the sort of thing that suits him, and to which he was born, so to speak. The symbolic power of the "Massey" microphone, however, determines the next and crucial moment in both this confession, and in Yasch's personal future in Gutenthal.

This moment confirms Yasch's utter individualism. It provides a sudden window on his particular, constructed character. We are given insights both into his relative honesty as well as into the nature of the Mennonite church (and of course the church in general, official institutions of any sort in general). We must remember, approaching this passage, that Yasch consistently portrays himself as an honest man who "gribbles" until he discovers the truth about a certain individual, about the church, or about a decision he must make. Now, consider Armin Wiebe's particular setup of the confession.

> It sure is different looking at the church from behind the pulpit. The whole church full is looking you on. And you are higher than everybody. And everybody you can see. And it's almost like you can see what everybody is thinking, because you can see their faces. Oata is there, her face shining like the sun. (143)

Great power resides in that place behind the pulpit. The man or woman there stands in a site of privilege. He sees everyone; he knows each of them in an intimate way. Oata, for instance (in a rare lyrical passage, English in its Anglo-Saxon syntax and rhythms), looks up at him, bright-eyed and true, "her face shining like the sun."

But the others, at least many of them, get off less lightly in this new light shining on them from the eyes of this anti-preacher, this false preacher, a "dow-nix" temporarily holding the reins of power.

> Forscha Friesen is there, and he looks nervous, but he looks like he wants to laugher himself, too. Dola Dyck is there, sitting in the second row, but I can't find the preacher that was him with. I look the rows down. Ha Ha Nickel is sitting Pug Peters and Sadie beside. Zoop Zack Friesen, who usually to the free church goes. Hauns Jaunses' Fraunz. Schlax Wiebe.

> Knibble Thiessen, the rightmaker. Fuchtig Froese. Store Jansen's Willy. Yelttausch Yeeatze. Penzel Panna and his girl-friend from Altwiese. Rape Rampel. Milyoon Moates. Hingst Heinrichs. Gopher Goosen.
>
> And on the women's side the women—Muttachi, her wet eyes glancing the light off like sparks—and the girls like Shtramel Stoesz and her sister Shups, that me and Hova Jake took to a crusade in Dominion City once. And the children in the front bench, waiting. And I see Klaviera Klassen sitting sideways on her piano bench and she is looking me on with such eyes that I have to look away . . . (143)

He knows them all, these people he communes with, for better or worse. All of them wait now for his words. Unlike the words of anyone before him at this place of power, Yasch's words touch all the hearts there. They are the languages they have encountered, largely the languages concerning the farm, the prairie, the livestock they raise, the sex they make evenings and mornings in the middle of their busy working daily worlds, the trips to "Winnipeg in the basement," Eaton's *em tjalla*, as I recall Mennonites calling it.

Their names especially give their materiality away. Yasch sees Oata, the big girl, who brings Yasch lunch on the field, her blouse unbuttoned and flying wide open in the wind. She drives a combine, loves eating ice-cream at the Dairy Dell. She takes her "honeymoon" in Winnipeg, travelling there in a pickup truck pulling a honeywagon (manure spreader). She is the one laughed at and rejected by kids in school. It is about her that the students, including Yasch, who pens the English version, write this terrible, earthy verse:

> Pissed in the water
> Hit a catter
> Pulled herself the panties down
> Found a lump there nice and brown
> Thought it was a Easter egg
> Rolled it up and down her leg
> Tasted first a tiny bit
> Holy cow it is just shit (58)

Ha Ha Nickel, also in the audience, is the rich farmer who entices Yasch to notice his daughter Sadie driving the tractor on the field with her blouse off and wearing only a black brassiere ("'Look out for the crows, Yasch,' Ha Ha laughs and he slams down the fertilizer lid. 'Twa Corbies,' I say, louder than I mean," 49). Later, secretly worried about his daughter spending time with a hired hand "dow-nix" instead of some rich man's son, Nickel offers a hypocritical excuse. He claims that he worries that Yasch "will try something yet" (95) and fires him, effectively denying him access to Sadie, whom he loves to distraction. Nickel shows his true material intentions by letting Sadie go where she wishes and do what she likes with Pug Peters, who quickly "gets into her pants" on the "double dike" one evening after the very Christian Endeavor Evening at which Yasch is informed he will be required to give a testimony. Conveniently for Nickel, Sadie becomes pregnant by the well-connected Pug Peters. Mennonite Canadians, it seems, proud of their spirituality, act with a common, material self-interest when it comes to securing husbands for their daughters.

A reluctant member of the audience, appropriately named Zoop Zack ("Alcohol Sack") Friesen, earlier in the day, appropriately New Year's Day, rages at certain visiting mummers and finds himself in consequence *brumtupped* (spooked) into attending church from then on. Among the more willing church members we find Hauns Jaunses' Fraunz. His nickname's alliterative punning, excessive and playful with language, places Mennonites willy nilly in the realm of the visceral. Despite the official will of ministers, councillors, bishops, elders, choir leaders, deacons, women's sewing circle leaders, and so on, these names show the reader that the Mennonite soul is stout, gay, and rambunctious.

Yasch exposes now, following the catalogue of members seated expectantly before him, not the hypocrisy of the church. He brings into light not his own hypocritical claim—a discourse based in large part on his performance in this confession—to represent honesty, with the others representing dishonesty. Instead, he exposes for all to see, not the sins of Forscha Friesen, but Forscha's "real" and desiring subjectivity, as the succeeding account of his crimes makes plain.

During the confession, Yasch recalls his schoolboy past when Forscha and his human "horses" stampede through the wiener roast of a group of good kids. They tie gentle Emmanuel to a tree and, while he accepts all they do to him with the long-suffering expected from someone with his name, the others, forced by Forscha's gang, spit on Emmanuel's face and revile him. Even Yasch, deeply respectful of Emmanuel, who shows no fear of Forscha, cannot in the end keep from participating in the torture, with his arm twisted behind his back by Melvin, who at the same time squeezes his testicles till Yasch's tears come. Forscha makes all of them, girls and boys both, touch and stroke Emmanuel's penis, which stiffens against his will (148).

Yasch confesses, but he confesses someone else's sins. Having confessed his sin as the product of the wrong Forscha did to Emmanuel, Yasch has not confessed but hypocritically exposed another's "sins." No one from this moment on will be able to relate as easily to Forscha without remembering his sins, no one will ever trust Yasch again to speak in an official capacity without opening the door to the skeletons in Gutenthal's closets, and no one will ever be able to enter the church again with the same complacency and the same sense of its sacred power over the "Devil." Yasch's confession regroups them, reforms them all. His confession, untrue, monological, material, reterritorializes (recodifies) the community by first deterritorializing (decodifying) it. Bringing the community to an understanding of its "sinfulness," meaning, in truth, its materiality, it nevertheless eventually rallies everyone around the common purpose of shunning Yasch. Chapters Nine and Ten of the novel clearly indicate how such a community, reterritorialized (recommitted) in their insistence on the evil of the poor and outspoken and disruptive, and on the good of the secretive, quiet, and obedient, always has to be hypocritical to protect God's status in their midst. Had they listened to Yasch, they would have had to abandon community, as Mennonites know it. Turning on him (while still respecting him at a material level, a level not easily allowed to speak in its reality), the church body (odd term) gives itself the gift of longevity and permanence. As in Rudy Wiebe's *Peace Shall Destroy Many*, reterritorialization comes at the cost of honesty and vulnerability. The community is saved. The salvation that Yasch Siemens delivers to Gutenthal is the salvation of a continued ontological (transcendent) perspective, which refuses to recognize the reality of its own onticality (earthliness), its constructedness. In other words, Yasch sacrifices himself in his "honesty" as the lamb that binds the large community ever more strongly in its group-held claims of divine purpose and sacred mission, and its refusal to see what is most transparent to a reader of Wiebe's artistic rendering of that group, its highly mischievous, selfish, cantankerous, joyful, celebratory, perversely vain and in every way material, discursive subjectivity.

4.

Growing a Mennonite Poet:
Patrick Friesen among the Raspberries

Pat Friesen is Mennonite Canada's first poet. He writes as if the reader had never before seen evidence of the inner workings and complexities of Mennonite Canadian life. As history text, non-Mennonites know the Mennonite world, as radio sermon they also know it, as articles and editorials in religious journals, as cookbook, as map, oral story (as jokes, for instance, in the *Mennonite Mirror, The Red River Valley Echo* or *The Pembina Times*), letters, martyrology (*The Martyrs' Mirror*), newspaper (*The Steinbach Post* or *The Altona Echo*), government document, sociology text, and photographic study, many experience it. As poetry, however, Mennonite Canada remains still undiscovered. Here, their politics and community values remain obscure.

I would like to begin this examination of Friesen's political poetry with a look at *bluebottle*, the second of his ten books. Its opening poems are lyrical. Thematically, they treat the phenomenon of the sudden, terrible beginning of the process of the growth of a poet. The persona, a young Mennonite male, experiences a traumatic "conversion" of sorts, following the death of his father.

bluebottle

he died on a stone pillow
his hand on a bannister
there was nothing between us

    for the moment

I was the staircase and the last touch
he the debut
between touch and ghost

I heard a bluebottle in the blind

    the droning was summer days
    chewing the stems of lilac leaves

    the fall of yellow afternoons

    suns glinting
    on the blue hood of our '53 dodge
    and father hoisting me
    to the hot fender for a photograph

    sitting still
    and father brushing sandflies off my back

    between touch and ghost
    while I heard time
    everything happened at once (9)

He converts not from paganism to Christianity (darkness to light
in traditional Neoplatonism), but from non-poet to poet. The
first six poems of *bluebottle* construct none of this "becoming-
poet" materially, openly, or on a literal level, but instead lyrically, imagistically, which is to say, indirectly. The poet makes
intense use of the objective correlative to present that particular,
critical moment in his poet's life when he comes to the decision
to take over his father's authority for paternal "law." He will
become "ghost" to take responsibility for "touch."

At a material level of the poem, we learn very little. We do
know that the poem features a bluebottle fly, at least if we go by
the title. We learn furthermore of someone's recent death. We
notice also the persona's cryptic comment about his oblique

involvement in that death. The persona—the poet, from now on—hears a fly in the blinds, or at least some sort of droning (the bluebottle's buzzing). The narrator claims that he hears time ("time's wing'd chariot," of course, if the reader recalls Marvell, but at a material level this allusion would not occur to readers) and then the poem ends. It is not much of a poem, really, if read at its most plain, most material level.

A much more sophisticated level exists within it, however. We interpret the poem to greater effect if we read metaphorically. In "bluebottle," and the other first half-dozen of the book's poems, the theme of the dying father dominates. "Bluebottle" tells of the poet coming to an important personal decision *because* of the death of his father. The opening line of "bluebottle," and so the line that determines the development of the ideas of the poem, explains that the father ("he") has "died on a stone pillow." Immense significance depends on "stone pillow." This poem and the ones that follow describe the process of the son taking over authority from his father. If we recall the story in Genesis to which the "stone pillow" directs our attention, we know that this modern poet takes upon himself a specific authority, the right to determine the future of his people. In Friesen's case, unlike that of Jacob, Abraham's grandson, this right takes the shape of "author," writing and rewriting the word in order to show his Mennonite people what it means to be their poet. Taken without irony, the biblical connection implies that the poet's people live in a foreign land, in a Canaan, in imminent danger of losing their communal identity. Someone must turn the people's inclinations away from Canaan worship and back towards its own traditions. Someone must again, as the story of Isaac and Jacob in Genesis tells us, "take a wife" from among the distant members of their Israelite clan in order to return the people to social roots and traditions, and so to multiply their seed in the world as God has promised Abraham via the sacred covenant, not unlike Tiddy Lang's despairing gloss of the state of gender relationships in Robert Kroetsch's *What the Crow Said*. To Gus Liebhaber's surprise, Tiddy inexplicably whispers, "Someone must take a wife," when she enters the pub in Indian Head and sees sitting there the passive John Skandle, local icemaker, her later lover, Gus Liebhaber, the printer and editor of the local paper who has just remembered a death that will take place that afternoon, as well as Tiddy's husband, whom she has come, in vain it turns out, to retrieve from the pub in the afternoon where the men have already, so early in the day, almost drunk themselves into a stupor.

The reference to the stone pillow implies the literary convention of receiving the mantle of poetry from a predecessor (a mentor). With this allusion Friesen invokes the history of the transmission of the biblical, patriarchal word and the blessing of special sons by dying fathers. In the biblical narrative of the stone pillow, Isaac in his old age calls his favourite son Jacob to him and commands him to travel to the distant land of Padanaram to find a wife among his own people, from "the house of Bethuel thy mother's father" (Genesis 28:2). Esau, the disgraced, sedentary, older brother to Jacob (a hunter, "Diana-like," moony and self-absorbed), discovers indirectly that his father dislikes Canaanite women; and he attempts, in bitterness, after the fact and in vain, to wring a blessing from Isaac, too. It is not to be, however. Isaac declares Jacob the blessed son, and prophesies to him that God will "make thee fruitful, and multiply thee, that thou mayest be a multitude of people" (Genesis 28:3). The biblical passage about the chosen son's experience with the stone pillow strongly explicates Friesen's "bluebottle" poem, particularly in the depiction of a staircase reaching to heaven with angels climbing up and down it.

> And he lighted upon a certain place, and tarried there all night, because the sun was set; and he took of the stones of that place, and put *them for* his pillows, and lay down in that place to sleep. And he dreamed, and behold a ladder set up on the earth, and the top of it reached to heaven: and behold the angels of God ascending and descending on it. (Genesis 28:11-12)

In this vision of the future, the visionary Jacob sleeps on a stone pillow and lives; the poet's father dies on the stone pillow. Think here also of Kroetsch's *Stone Hammer* poems and their return to the story of the vision implicit in the stones of our beginnings: of the biblical connection between stone and leadership, stone and vision, and by extension, stone and poetry (stone and story). This idea gets written later in stone, so to speak, in *Seed Catalogue,* where the question "How do you grow a poet?" echoes through the work like the careful blows of a sculpting hammer; Galatea the emerging poet under the loving blows of the philosopher sculptor. The father, in Friesen's poem, then has been a type of failed prophet, one prophet of the word among all the ones over the last four thousand years who have brought the message of God's covenant to his chosen people. Whereas Jacob sleeps on the stone pillow and lives to produce the seed of a multitude of his people, in contrast, the poet is his dead father's seeding. Where Jacob's story tells of the survival of fathers, the poet's story concerns the dying of fathers. This theme of lost fathers clearly troubles Friesen since at least the poem "fathers die" in the earlier book, *the lands i am.* If the living father is responsible for the seed, for the future of his people, then it is the living son of the dead father who carries a similar responsibility. These two scenarios differ starkly. The first, the biblical one, keeps the weight of duty on the father, the second takes it off the father who absconds, and makes the young, tender, timid, weak one bear what his father has too easily relinquished. The second is a reluctant visionary, ironically, an Esau, in effect.

A brief analysis of the first half dozen poems in Friesen's *the lands i am* clarifies some of the poet's intentions in the second book, *bluebottle.* Common knowledge tells us the dead father is a Freudian theme involving the ambitions and the process of individuation of a son challenging his father and separating from his mother. Laius is killed by his son, Oedipus, who must find a way of marrying the mother (the community). This theme of overthrowing the father and sympathizing with the nurturing mother holds for many of Friesen's books. When someone overthrows his father, that someone takes over his authority. The now dead, once visible "God" (father) of this universe must be replaced by a new God, since no corner of the world may, or even can, go unordered in the Oedipal myth. In Friesen's prairie world, where no models for such new ordering exist except European ones, the poet places himself temporarily in charge of the dispensation of fatherly wisdom.

sun king again

I'll be staunch
subdue the rabble
and be aristocrat again

be king
for a moment
. . . .
for a moment
I am king
and king governs
the lands I am (5)

Notice Friesen's literary intellectuality; he subtly employs the
great old model of the "false king" who, self-serving, deprecates
his choice to temporarily stand in for a king. The second book of
Paradise Lost begins with Satan's spurious claim that by taking
temporary kingship he serves and protects his "rabble" by plac-
ing his person between God's wrath and the defenseless fallen
angels. Dryden's "Mac Flecknoe" contains a memorable scene in
which the hero of that satirical piece places on the throne that
son "who most resembles me" and who will "reign, and wage
immortal war on wit" (904). In Friesen's poem, cockiness and
self-satisfaction characterize this fledgling king. An "aristocrat,"
he rules with a stern hand to "subdue the rabble." "Regency"
derives from an earlier age. This word may connote, however,
any other time period besides ours, even one current with the life
of Jonah, the reluctant prophet who resists being God's poet, his
voice of truth. God overcomes Jonah's reluctance with various
trials, among them Leviathan swallowing him and eventually
spitting him out on dry land after four days. Friesen's second
poem here, "Jonah," precisely describes the dilemma of the poet
who wishes not to be held responsible for the word.

why do I go into this secret room
with my bowels churning?
. . . .
to seize three or four words
which I lack. (6)

These lines clearly describe the sentiments of most biblical visionaries, all of whom prefer not to have to take up words they lack. The Bible recounts no stories of naturally loquacious prophets. Moses, for instance, even seeing the burning bush and other signs of God's support, pleads not to have to endure speaking for Him.

The third poem of *the lands i am* takes us out of biblical times to 1685 and the martyrdom of Margaret Wilson, burned at the stake, singing praises as the flames devour her. Both the poet and the martyr "sing" in the face of persecution. Though she dies in Europe, still she inspires us here and in a powerfully Canadian way, since her dust, her ashes, have blown over all lands. She has become "the scattered silt / of three centuries living" (7). If the poet, scratching for words to describe the lands he is, fears that he lacks models for his writing, he need only turn to this woman's image, to the understanding that the soil of the earth— even soil of the Canadian prairies—holds a secret knowledge of all suffering and strength. Continuing his historic journey, Friesen's fourth poem in the book, "Nestor Makhno: anarchist," takes us forward in time, closer to the poet's home, specifically to the Russian persecution of Mennonites in the late nineteenth and early twentieth centuries. These Mennonites experience a torture as devilish as Margaret Wilson's. In the next of the poem's images, Friesen describes the Mennonites aboard the Teutonia enduring a miserable, two-week-long crossing. Finally, the Atlantic spanned, the poet's ancestors arrive in a foreign country where they "must," in terror, begin to build a new culture. The "must" implies the fear involved in such a pursuit, one barked into them by the unfamiliarity of the new place. (Thought tells us that the new inhabitants would go through a variety of religio-political contortions in order to force the new place into blocks and structures suitable to their own old world beliefs. Atwood's *The Journals of Susanna Moodie* explores just this thought. Our social formations in the new land all derive from the fearful.)

The fifth poem, "culture building," describes the multiplicity of groups and traditions that construct the poet himself, from the Aboriginal/French Métis culture, the British explorer Samuel Hearne's culture, to that of the Roman soldiers and the Russian military whose terrible scythes "hacked twitching embryos/

from swollen bodies" (10). After this horrible reminder of history's bloody legacy, the poems no longer derive from foreign subject matter, but from the poet's personal territory, the Canadian prairie around Steinbach, Manitoba, a stony land worked by his forefathers. Finally home, in the multicultural place he recognizes as his own, the poet feels free to write what concerns him most passionately, his people here in Canada, his immediate family's interrelationships, a concern that possibly finds its strongest expression in "fathers die" The poems in *the lands i am* thus quickly move from the distant biblical past through time and history up to the present moment and the death of the poet's father. This backward look at the politics and history of his people, a history always concerned with place and filiation, authenticates in a classical way the poet's present resolve to write, and to write specifically about place, namely "prairies" (*the lands i am* 10) and Oedipal suffering.

Now, in *bluebottle*, the dying father takes centre stage. The fathers dying in Genesis and on the prairie share many qualities, but differ much, too. The phrase "his hand on a bannister" begins to explain how the Mennonite poet is his father's seeding. A bannister, of course, forms part of a staircase. A staircase appears to Jacob in his dream, a dream portending his future importance to the history of man. Man, this patriarch learns, will be connected to heaven and heaven's beings through Jacob's marriage to a kinswoman, and thus a marriage to the future of the covenant that "the people" will continue to worship Yahweh and Yahweh will continue to consider them his people. The stairway ("I was the staircase and the last touch") symbolizes the connection between God and man, a connection tradition tells us a few chosen men ensure. Abraham is covenanted to be the human connection first; Isaac next, with his marriage to the lovely Rachel; Isaac chooses Jacob to continue the great "poetic" sacred planting, growing, generating; Jacob passes the blessing on to one of his sons; eventually the seed of Abraham proliferates and the covenant grows and strengthens in proportion to the increase of God's people, products of that original promise made to Abraham.

Unexpectedly, instead of seeing the God-sent vision and interpreting it for those who follow, the poet's father "die[s] on a stone pillow" (9). He fails to make life out of the stone pillow experience as Jacob has done, as those few chosen in every generation to carry the covenant on must do to be visionaries. "His hand on a bannister" further suggests the meaning that the father fixes his eyes on the staircase to heaven, and considers a possible attempt at climbing it, or interpreting it, but somehow irresolute, manages no more than to simply grasp its bannister before he dies. At this point, the suggestive term "us" comes into play. The poet quietly involves himself in the image of the staircase and the stone pillow: "there was nothing between us," he says, suggesting an absence of relationship, a "nothing" (9), between father and son. If the father died at the gate to "truth," or vision, the son's task involves a greater accomplishment, to attempt that which will be more, that which will be "nothing" like his father did. "Nothing" might also mean simply, "that which is still not something." In this sense, the words imply a temporary non-substantiality, which some forthcoming event might suddenly alchemize. In the problematization of touch and ghost here, is the shadow of the old poetical convention of the alchemist and alchemy, the turning of dross into gold through mystical means, through incantation mixed with science. The introduction of touch and ghost, with the specifics of the discussion *that* dichotomy inspires, neatly directs us to think of "nothing" in this sense of imminent transformation, as an absence which is about to become a touch and that this becoming will happen as a result of a shift in the poet's perspective. All these complexities concerning the Mennonite poet's sense of relative touch and ghostliness are only suggested through symbol, conveyed in a "ghostly" way through modes of intense elision. We see here, then, the exact *modus operandi* of the lyric with its methods based on secrecy and restraint—elision is applied secrecy and restraint—really a sort of nothing, a failure of vision.

The shift from nothing between us to something between us happens elsewhere, outside this poem. Nothing existed between us "for the moment," the poet thinks, separating the lines before "for the moment" and after it with large spaces as if to draw special attention to these words, saying, in effect, "They stand out like this from the rest because they indicate the main point of the poem, that I am no longer in a non-relationship with my father (as I was in 'fathers die'), nor am I in a defined and new relationship with him, but I am here in the front parlor of our house, in a critical balance and temporary stasis which will determine my future. I am here where Father lies prior to the funeral ceremonies. What a momentous decision, to decide to lead a people, to act as the spokesman for a people and its visionary tie to the sacred covenant."

Clearly, the decision remains unmade by the young man, most likely standing there in the room with the coffin, in the immediacy of experiencing his father's death. That decision comes at some later time. The poem's effective use of the past voice ("I was the staircase"; "I heard a blueblottle"; "he died") establishes the importance of *reflection* in the poet's eventual discovery of how the death and the funeral mark him somehow as a poet before he understands it has done so. He analyzes the event further. Not only is he in stasis at the time, immobilized by the death, but he responds to the events around him in a way peculiar to the poetic imagination. He responds to the death not directly, through touching the dead face and hands, or through a detailed exploration of memories of the two of them at some intimate game or work, or through abstract utterances of love and loss such as, "Oh, Father, you never should have left me," but through a series of such intense objective correlatives as Pound, Eliot, Hulme, H.D., Richards, Leavis, Brookes, and the other eminent instructors of the twentieth century poetic consciousness have successfully taught as *the* aesthetic to Friesen's age. According to literary modernism, poetry of quality necessarily produces a single, sharp moment of understanding in the reader by means of a powerful image, by means of the substitution of rare and more difficult objective images for common subjective statements of feeling and intent.

The poet, thinking about the boy standing there by the coffin, recalls how he responds to the following events. He *senses* the following things without thinking. He hears a trapped bluebottle fly, buzzing, approaching its own death between the drawn blind darkening the death room and the bright, hot, sunlit window pane. The stationary bluebottle ineffectually buzzes, stuck between past and future, much like the bereaved son. He is trapped where light will kill him, though bluebottles sometimes buzz in vain in apparent agony in the blinds for days. The window blind (blind poet, blind uncertainty, blind necessity, blindness to codes and traditions, blindness to the future) impedes things, separates and forces confrontations. The sun confronts the window blind and gets turned back from its natural affect of lighting the room. The sun confronting the blind makes for a highly provocative, layered image here, considering Friesen's decades-long, common artistic equation of the sun with paternal authority, and "heavenly" light with viciousness—as I will take pains to show—two patterns given only to an earth-blinded poet, accustomed to the dark, accustomed to seeing without light (Teiresias). The darkness of the death room remains, unmediated by the sun because of the blind. Only that which finds itself between the dark room and the bright outside spaces experiences entrapment in a place where it sees and senses both what the dark room holds and what the sun's world shows. The bluebottle poet senses as well as sees from the spot where he finds himself cornered by his particular relationship with his father. *He* is "the staircase" (9), which his father, dying on the stone pillow, not able to go on, vainly grasps in his hand. *He* is "the last touch," the last thing his father touches, "the debut / between touch and ghost" (9), and touched in this sacred way by ancestral, patriarchal, religious history, the bluebottle poet becomes a ghost to reality. He becomes a ghost to immediate experience and that sense of the real humans often define in terms of touch, for in this room, so soon after *this* father's death, he already begins to turn subjective "reality" and touch (the truths, codes, and abstractions we territorialized ones find ourselves in touch with) into the "ghostliness" of objective correlatives, of images, of lyric, symbolic, metaphoric pictures. I say the "ghostliness of objects" because the pictures not familiar to others (of the prairie instead of imagined heaven) will be familiar to him; the reality of objects he touches with love will be ghostly, peripheral things to his people, hypocritically accustomed (as I claim in my analysis of Rudy Wiebe's and Armin Wiebe's works) to spiritual realities which, inversely, he, the poet, will find ghostly.

I suggest with this close reading of "bluebottle," which nevertheless only scratches its lyrical surface, that Friesen extensively understands the lyrical. He uses it with remarkable facility. The poet's mastery of conventional poetics is not, however, a sign of satisfaction with the lyrical style. Precisely the opposite holds true, I think. Friesen demonstrates his lyrical mastery in order to indicate frustration with it. He purposes not to hide all evidence of the lyrical in his work, but, rather, to illuminate the struggle he as a poet in Canada, on the prairie, faces in his desire to "represent" himself, and his people, and their experiences. How does the chosen poet write after Europe? How does he write or unwrite the lyric, with its density of symbol and its massive restraint, in a land that counsels its subjects to wait and listen ("heard a bluebottle"), and not always already have standing something between the subject and the moment? How can the poet write against the received wisdom of the lyrical with its long, Euro-English semantic history, with its predictable system of meanings, and long-baked, cleverly transmitted, potently binding moral structures? That conundrum buzzes in the blind, caught between touch and ghost; that is what is blindly trapped by the light through the death-room window; that is what the poet feels compelled to covenant with his father to write about:

> I smelled heat
> off the pavement
> saw it shimmer
> above the field
>
> I was there
> his accomplice
> among idle worshippers
> who would not let go
>
> I heard the buzzing of a bottled fly ("accomplice" 15)

This poem segment derives (in the lyrical tradition of the colossal restraint of allusion) from and drives further the implications of Yeats's "The Lake-Isle of Innisfree." Friesen tells us *more* about "pavement" than Yeats, but with fewer words, fewer "bee-loud glade" constructions. Friesen, if anything, demonstrates how suggestively elisive is his skill. Here the poet is his father's accomplice. He is not his father's enemy. Not *only* his enemy, at least. If he is his enemy, a great task unites him with his enemy more than it separates. This uniting with the enemy in a common goal forms the crux of the Christian message, after all. The Christian subject is to love his enemy as himself. So the poet in his partnership with his father, between whom and himself "there is nothing for this present moment," announces his Christian duty, a burden of sorts, to "feed" the buzzing fly in him, to not eat the traditional sacerdotal bread of the Eucharist with its two-thousand-year-old "unChristian" traditions, but to rewrite this world and these traditions represented by his father with whom he feels, and in a moment swears, a complicity.

> bread was flesh of the dead
> I could not eat
>
> later
> in the basement
> of the house he built
> i whispered my rites (15)

The poet cannot eat the flesh of the dead, cannot take the father in as dead, fears the earth and its warm decadence. In effect, though he attends the funeral ("I was at the funeral"), though he sings communally with the singing Mennonites ("their amazing grace / made me weep for old days"), and though he has "consented" to all the last wishes of the dying man ("father died / wanting to die / I consented / and felt his blessing"), he finds it impossible to face the earthy facts of death. The poet can consent to the death, can deal with the words of the blessing, but when it comes to the actual signs of the flesh and its mouldering, he can go no further and must find ways of substituting word for flesh, spirit for body. In this fear of the dead body and commitment to the living word in the place of death ("in the basement / of the house he had built"), he dramatizes the biblical incarnation.

> He came unto his own, and his own received him not. But as many as received him, to them gave he power to become the sons of God, *even* to them that believe on his name: Which were born, not of blood, nor of the will of the flesh, nor of the will of man, but of God. And the Word was made flesh, and dwelt among us, (and we beheld his glory, the glory of the only begotten of the Father,) full of grace and truth. (St. John 1:11-14)

I quote the passage in full because it echoes *bluebottle*. The two texts share the theme of difference from others; in Friesen's case, from Mennonites, his people, but who differ from him in beliefs and understanding. A similar awkward separateness also informs the message, "He came unto his own [people], and his own received him not." In "accomplice" we see, in this light, the young man at the funeral with his Mennonite brethren, conscious of his difference from them.

> I was at the funeral
>
> all the brethren
> my stiff-necked mennonites
> carried the coffin
> and sang
>
> their amazing grace
> made me weep for old days (15)

Their amazing grace (graciousness, dignity) reminds him of something lost, something from the old days when, as a youngster, he sang the old songs and recited the old religious ideas with belief. Their *singing* of "Amazing Grace," however, reminds him of olden days and traditions lost to all Mennonites. What they have lost can only be recovered or discovered by the poet gradually, over time, if he commits himself to that arduous task for a lifetime, an intention the poet announces at the end of this poem with "whispered ... rites." The difference between them and him concerns something lost on both their parts, and by implication, something each has in its power to give the other. Herein lies the reason for his turning to words and not to flesh ("blood"). It concerns the "chosenness" of the special son to bring truth to a people reluctant to hear, the complicity between father and son, the preference for words instead of earth and blood. In "whispering these rites" to write about and write out of the father's world, a Mennonite traditional religious world, the poet commits himself to a life of interpolating the buzzing bluebottle between the blinding light of the sun and the warming material world of the dark, warm grave.

a pastor's prayer is a momentary span
that dissolves in open air

a loam mound warms in the sun ("graveside" 11)

This dark earth/bright sun binary—lyrical binary—persists in Friesen's work. The two halves complicate and direct the flow of ideas in much of Friesen's poetry for the next dozen years. The insistent presence of earth/sun imagery informs *The Shunning* most fully and with the greatest subtlety of all his works.

Bluebottle analyzes the inverted realities of Mennonite spirituality and a hypocritical (though consciously non-hypocritical, what they themselves would call "realistic," or "the most realistic reality of all which is and is all about heaven") community more individualistic than social. The image that opens "accomplice" strongly implies this unthoughtful individualism. The poem's specific subjected group is Mennonite, whose personal as well as religious attitudes toward individuals of other cultures and each other is proud and stubborn ("stiff-necked"). When they sing at the funeral they sing very well, with a peculiar grace for which their singing has long been noted. Local *sängerfests*, local church choirs, the Canadian Mennonite University's perennial and gifted mixed choir, soloists such as Ben Heppner and Henriette Schellenberg, the general involvement of Mennonites in all music programs at all levels of accomplishment, provincial, national, and international, provide living proof of the grace Friesen notices and inscribes. He himself feels "stiff-necked" proud of this gift in his people. Much more to his point, however, is the fact that, religiously speaking, the Mennonite acts with less graciousness when relating to others than when making music: the poem writes that they sing *their* "Amazing Grace," not anyone else's version of it. An aspect of Mennonite spirituality that has long been a cause of suffering among its people, old and young, is its acceptance and insistence upon that most puritan of sentiments about the religious subject which "Amazing Grace" enshrines—that the individual is a guilt-bound, sin-ridden, worthless creature whom God somehow sees fit to love, regardless. "Amazing grace, how sweet the sound / that saved a wretch like me," the song goes, revealing its sentimental connection with another puritan bastion, the seventeenth century novel

Robinson Crusoe. In it the luckless Robinson finally discover the true goodness of Providence in isolating him on his uninhabited island, which he has understood till this moment of revelation to be its indifference to him:

> *Why has god done this to me? What have I done to be thus used?*
> My conscience presently checked me in that inquiry, as if I had blasphemed, and methought it spoke to me like a voice: "WRETCH! dost thou ask what thou hast done? Look back upon a dreadful misspent life and ask thyself what thou hast not done; ask, Why is it that thou wert not long ago destroyed? (82)

The individual Christian subject for Crusoe and for the Puritans is a wretch whose conscience, if the subject listens to it, will invert a blithe sense of personal blamelessness and turn it into an authentic and proper self-denial and self-disgust, which eventually then returns the gift of a new heavenly bliss. This bliss, however, is bodiless, not of this world, stiff-necked in its insistence on the reality of the spirit and the false, lying, deceitful unreality of the material world.

This digression concerning the wretched subject of "Amazing Grace" illustrates Mennonite hypocritical reality. In "accomplice" it works in this way: at the very home of the material, the grave, the stiff-necked Mennonites in their blessed voices cannot sense, cannot let themselves feel, the dark *welcome* of earth, the "loam mound" which "warms in the sun" (11). Friesen's Mennonite poet cannot, either. He, too, he realizes with discomfort, is an inverter. Poetry represents for him an inversion of the material into something other, something of pictures rather than of objects. He is, after all, an "accomplice" who wishes he were not that, who, for dramatic effect, to jolt his senses into being sense, climbs closer to, and metaphorically deeper into, the sensual grave by descending into the basement to "whisper [his] rites" (15). The basement is man-made and so a compartmentalized, ordered bunker more than a loam mound: the poet's is a wishful, ineffectual journey into the grave, into the underworld; a false harrowing of hell. The word itself—the poetic word and the non-poetic word, these whispered rites hopeful of reuniting the poet to the earth, and later hopeful of uniting his people to the earth of their past, to their material past—denies the material and constitutes a forced, vain singing of "Amazing Grace." The whispered rites in the basement are the gentle, quiet, tentative words of commitment to his calling, in his father's house, in the site of patriarchal authority proper to the commitment to God's work of a Jacob or a Moses. The poet speaks "quiet" words because the poet is embarking on a career that stiff-necked Mennonites discourage and which, regardless, takes much courage and an odd mixture of arrogance and humility. The calling that chooses him requires him to sing a new version of "Amazing Grace" that will not carry a coffin, that will not carry its own death around with it. His vision calls him to return his people's gaze from self-loathing and stubborn sun-inspired spirituality to a new materiality.

He is chosen against his will. "Jonah" has hinted this, the very progress of the poems of *the lands i am* have strongly suggested this, "bluebottle" more than suggested it with its complex "stone pillow" image, and now another poem describes it even more explicitly. "Whispered basement rites" speaks of a particular meaning of "chosen." It means that his calling will be to bring his "stiff-necked mennonites" a new ritual acquaintance with the earth. That he is *chosen* to bring a new vision of the material vividly presents itself to the reader in the stunning poem "mother," which appears early in Friesen's fourth book, *Unearthly Horses*:

mother

1.
her bare feet in dust
holding her print dress above the knees
she sprints toward home   laughing

2.
a girl in her summer dress
sun shifting through foliage   on her yellow hair
father   his arm around her waist   crooning wilf carter

3.
in the garden
leaning on her hoe
pushing back strands of hair
her eyes lock on mine
where i lie on my stomach
between rows of raspberry bushes

this is how I was chosen

4.
ma singing me to sleep
with 'the golden vanity'
and sailing dreams of 'sir patrick spens'
telling me gypsies she remembered
greasy skirts and pans   their fire and paint
at the edge of altona their dance   (5)

That is how he was chosen. He will sing the earth, to which he persistently draws near in his memories of the past ("where i lie on my stomach / between rows of raspberry bushes," for instance). His whispered rites in the basement to sing the earth echo the earth and sea songs he remembers his mother singing to him at bedtime.

The songs his mother sings pertain closely now to the themes that preoccupy Friesen later. "Golden vanity," for example, warns him early of the pride of the sun. The sun features as the quintessential symbol in Friesen's poetry. It always blinds Mennonites or freezes them with its cold, fierce light. For Friesen, the sun represents the non-material, hypocritical spiritual that divides his people from pleasure and love. Gold, the colour and affect in the heavens of the sun, traditionally opposes the dark, and stands in the classical sense for an old cosmology that calls the earth corrupt. For religion and the Ptolemaics, heaven, furthermore, is the place of true gold, of refined and refining light.

For Friesen, the sun and light stand for a dehumanizing, desocializing spiritualism. None of his books amass more evidence of this view than *The Shunning.* At the point when Peter is sitting on his swing in his yard after the announcement by his church brethren of his excommunication, while he is beginning to contemplate suicide, he hears the rooster on his brother's adjacent farm, crowing in the separating light.

rooster crows the sun
and I know what must be done
before it crows again (36)

Early in the morning, on his way to get his rifle, he kills all his
chickens in a grisly simultaneous affirmation and negation of the
material. He smells the rancidness of rotting eggs, as a reminder
both of the sensuality of which death deprives the subject, and of
the decay of life and life's pleasure in the material.

I dress quickly
walk out   boots in hand

running for the henhouse
I smell the heap of smashed eggs
grab the startled rooster and twist his neck
throw him on the stinking eggs

hens flutter as I flounder   reaching
tearing with my hands   my teeth
spitting blood and feathers
fat headless hens dancing on broken shells (36)

In the midst of this carnage, with the stink of the carrion's return
to dust, in the haste of his killing spree, the sun rises to call him
to his own death.

Greek art, again, Greek beauty, have their root in the same
impulse to see things as they really are, inasmuch as Greek art
and beauty rest on fidelity to nature—the best nature—and
on a delicate discrimination of what this best nature is. To say
we work for sweetness and light, then, is only another way of
saying that we work for Hellenism (Matthew Arnold,
"Culture and Anarchy" 2121).

The sun, religion with its truth and light, with its sweetness and
light as Matthew Arnold speaks of it here, is the same sun with
which the poet earlier claims a complicity and from which he cannot free himself. This complicity persistently and fearfully pits him
against the earth whose "bread was flesh of the dead / I could not
eat" (*bluebottle* 15). Mindless of the havoc, the sun now ruthlessly
beckons him to wake up to another day of human isolation and
social extirpation.

sun slants in at the windows
on the spattered floor   on my untied boots

from Johann's farm a cock crows
the sun will not be denied (36)

Of course, the crowing cock recalls the biblical Peter's denial of
Christ. In Friesen's text, Peter's social alienation is exponentially
greater still than his wife Helena's, who, dispirited with watching
her husband's declining sociability, sums up the nature of the
indifference of the sun in this way:

this distance will not be forgiven

I must come back
sit on benches
if I am to be loved again

but how do I come back? (37)

The great distance of their removal from love is both that from
their fellow church members and the vast separation from the
source of love their Mennonite brethren worship and in whose
name Peter has been singled out for shunning. Reverend Loewen
recalls Peter's whispered words at the moment the committee of
brethren confront Peter: "all this light he said / all this cold cold
light" (39). Moments before Peter's death, while he prays for
God to forgive "them" and "me" (41) the poet (not Peter) tells us
that "his [Peter's] brother shivers at noon" in uncanny telepathic
knowing, and with the sun at its most potent height. One day,
many years later, when Johann remembers all that Peter taught
him about life and death, the sun's cold power declines and the
earth suddenly replaces it in a powerful way. A new warmth
enters the world of *The Shunning*, a fertile and familial earth.

johann remembered his brother
who tore the curtain and went blind
who taught johann fear   and not fear
that the child dies no matter what
and a man carries his funeral with him
you never know how many people you bury with a man
nor how many are born again

come   said johann   let's go back to the house
ruth bakes bread today
it's good when it's still warm and the butter melts

listen   he whispered

that rasping sound   that's a yellowhead
see it   over there   near the creek

and I saw
a blackbird with a sun for its head (98)

This last (may I add, brilliant) poem in *The Shunning* points the
reader and the poet back to a former book and ahead toward his
next two books, closing a circle, so to speak, of poems that indicate the distance between sun and earth, namely between
Mennonite spirituality and Mennonite materiality. The delightful and welcoming image of a wife (Johann's second wife Ruth)
baking bread with butter melting on a slice of it beckons us back
to an old territorial world of Mennonite love of food, hearth,
earth, drink, socializing, and sex. Mennonite materiality contra-
dicts. It both affirms and negates life's celebration. Because this
moment occurs in Johann's revitalized world long after Peter's
death, we may read it as a reterritorialized more than a territorial world. *This*, this material, satisfying, social, non-stiffnecked
side of the Mennonite culture and personality constitute the
world the poet feels chosen to bring. It *is* the word he has "whispered" (*bluebottle* 15) to himself and his readers in his father's
basement that he will devote himself to write and so to
memorialize instead of that of the hypocritical sun. Here he says,
"listen he whispered," and we must recall the weight of meaning
the chosen poet has earlier placed on his "quiet" words, his fearful entry into complicity with his father, and his long, long
apprenticeship of silent, poetic ritual. Peter tearing the curtain
and going "blind" returns us to the bluebottle fly caught between
light and dark in the blind of the death room. "Rasping," in the
undertow of this baking bread image, reminds us suddenly of the
historical moment that "chose" the poet when he lay on the
ground between raspberry rows with his mother's eyes locked on
his (*Unearthly Horses* 5). "Yellowhead" and "a blackbird with a
sun for its head" send us to the title of his fifth book, *Flicker and*

Hawk. Flickers rasp at wood, sport yellow and black feathers, and yet here hardly represent the deceptive, cold world of the sun, which the poet religiously opposes over so many decades with images of earth and darkness.

The image of the yellow-headed blackbird that ends *The Shunning* mitigates the story of social distance and the church's exclusion. It combines, in a fine gesture of community, the golden ("vain") world of the sun his mother once warned him about, and the black, warm world of death to which Sir Patrick Spens goes, as we all know, part-way through his voyage of service for his king. Remember Friesen's earlier "I am King"? *The Shunning* ends by bringing the reader back to the material. No universal categories destine the sun to rule; the poet turns the tide of official territorial codes favouring the sun's rule by effectively telling a story of reterritorialization and recoding.

The chosen poet knows another spirituality besides the official spirituality of the sun. Official spirituality deceives. It calls to the poet and seduces him with a sense of its longevity and social possibility: the people, after all, believed in official versions of spirituality for four hundred years; their faith profoundly kept them a people:

> as they sing 'amazing grace'
> a dirge that moves me through time
> to whatever passed for eden
> I want to stand and say we are together
> blessing four hundred years with our names
> but I catch the lie
> and remember it was a young boy's eden
> mine alone   and I know who seared whom
> I know eden vanished before the cross
> ("easter morning 1966" *Unearthly Horses* 10)

The young man once idealized Eden, the place of early love, of first sex, of knowing. He now knows, however, despite the seduction of that old "Amazing Grace," that Eden offers nothing for him or for his people besides a "searing" hell and a legacy of ignorance and separation into gross, sad individuality. Eden, lovely and sensual, remains a dream of only one boy, not a commonly held vision of a free and material Adam and Eve, naked and young, naked and amazingly graceful in a gorgeous world.

This other grace, this other unofficial spirituality unlit by the sun, resides in places typically untrodden by Mennonite preachers.

letter to the brimstone church

I follow black caverns of jungle
everywhere I look grotesque shapes hang
distant barking nears and the dull pound of drums
I don't see the clearing until I am in it

at the centre a shallow ditch flames
a path of flat stones meanders across

fronds quiver and part
a procession enters the circle (*bluebottle* 19)

The poet descends into hell. He descends easily, without difficulty (broad is the way that leads to hell). Hell the material. The dark, fecund, cavernous jungle bulges with terrible shapes hanging from the high trees. The cavern is emblematically here a womb, given the subject matter and the rest of the poem's images of earth and sexuality. The heads of Cerberus bark, "distant barking nears"(19), drums pound as they do in Conrad's *Heart of Darkness* with its inky, impenetrable shores and its endless ignorance of the Aboriginal other (always cast in the absence of colour and the fulminating presence of eternal, pounding, drum rhythms).

The poet fearlessly—instinctively knowing from past literary experience that not damnation but only illumination awaits him in exciting sorties of this sort—crosses a ditch on a path of "flat" stones that "meander" across it. The onomatopoeic duplicity in "ditch" calls up by sound the strong sensations both of an ooze-filled slimy place, uninviting to human step, as well as an earthy site on the other hand, so much more tangible than anything in the history of the sky could possibly be. So far "hell" holds nothing all that dreadful for the poet explorer. Entry at its gates and progress further in beckon him on with their ease, with their passivity. Fire neither bursts nor flares, but simply, mildly, "flames"; and the poet makes the crossing without harrowing haste hurried on by dangers, but in a mood of slowness and, perhaps, grace.

What will come next, here in this place far from the sun and official goodness? Surely something fearful to the poet, something to justify all our straining to disembody our understandings and aspire upwards towards landless, sunny Platonic, Judeo-Christian immutability. Landless, sunny heaven contrasts Friesen's general meaning in the title of his first book. "The lands i am" plays on the sense of the landless (aspiring) world the Mennonite Canadian church—the "brimstone church"—would have him be: "fronds quiver and part / a procession enters the circle" (*bluebottle* 19).

The terrible secret of hell promises to reveal itself in a moment. The image at the moment of seeing is plainly sexual. His body in its forward movement parts the fronds obscuring his view. He peers into the eternal womb, into the world of the maternal. This is a world that angels, if we read Milton on heaven and earth, secretly and jealously wish to deny. This world heaven, the angels (spirits), and the "brimstone church" all spend their lives, their energies, and their imaginations denying, refusing, and preaching against, envious of the power of earth and especially of females to create life while males remain relegated to fighting and the production of great, deadly battles. All angels in heaven are male. In Milton's *Paradise Lost*, the only woman in heaven is Sin, and she is imagined and bodiless, springing from Satan's mind in a gross, airy parody of God's material woman. God's women, in contrast, He makes good, lovely, and fully creative like himself. In *Paradise Lost*, Raphael, stunned at Eve's ability to create, trained in and raised on hierarchy and rule, misunderstanding God's generosity and generative nature, counsels Adam to rule over Eve and subdue her passionate nature. Angels in heaven are not only male but also homosexual: to Adam's question about how angels love, whether "Express they, by looks only, or do they mix / Irradiance, virtual or immediate touch," Raphael answers him evasively, but blushing to high heaven. "To whom the Angel with a smile that glow'd / Celestial rosy red, Love's proper hue, / Answer'd. Let it suffice thee that thou know'st / Us happy, and without Love no happiness" (Book VIII, 618-21). Angels live, by implication, incapable of procreation. The realm of the sun, in other words, is a sterile one.

The poet "unfronds" a material, generative world. It is a place of great grace, a world of the mother whose love and yearning so many of Friesen's poems attempt to recreate: "young girls / slim and feathered like night-flowers / sleepwalk by me" (*bluebottle* 19). The girls, attractive, with all the blissful qualities of flowers, "sleepwalk by," both because this is the place of lethargy and forgetting in the mythic wisdom about hell, and because the image projects his sense of being in a dream-world, in a world he has not ever believed real. Friesen cares little to be original in the metaphor; it simply "does" in the best sense of material poetry, good enough for the required effect. Shakespeare's Hamlet, in a scene whose context I find curiously relevant to Friesen's poetry, listens to the words of his dead father, whose ghost comes up from hell to caution him about the horrors and dangers of hell:

> I find thee apt;
> And duller shouldst thou be than the fat weed
> That roots itself in ease on Lethe wharf
> Wouldst thou not stir in this. (*Hamlet* I.v.32-35)

The brimstone church never taught him this about hell, of course, never prepared him for hell's loveliness.

> I smell their moist spices
>
> I watch the first girl
> her breasts not yet budding
> hypnotic hips swaying
>
> I hear no incantation
> no signals given
> as she walks toward the stones
> her lithe arms rise
> undulate like charmed snakes
>
> each step she takes is easy and precise
> she is kelp dancing in a fiery sea (19)

Such seas, on fire, are yet not on fire. They burn without burning. They burn maybe in the way St. Paul cautioned against, but their fires "charm" and "hypnotize" more than they destroy. The maternal, the woman, the girl "who walks toward the stones," is *herself* snakes (plural, multiple) and not, by way of contrast, seduced by a singular, intelligent, and deadly advisor reptile who intends the destruction of "woman"; whose motive is hatred and jealousy of that mankind whom God created superior to all earth's creatures, and whose injunction official religion determined must be to "bruise thy head . . . [as] thou shalt bruise his heel" (Genesis 3:15). Here, the poet describes the stones, now with hell as context, and not a "stone-pillow" at the base of the staircase to heaven, as low and easy to cross. Stones here represent another sort of passage over than in Jacob's Genesis. The girl undulates like kelp; she sways with a natural, hypnotic seductiveness. No words in the poem "signal" danger at her movements and grace, in contrast to the Old Testament version, which proclaims with a sort of frenetic hurry against Eve's sojourn on earth. Hell provides no background dirge or chanted rites ("whispered rites," *bluebottle* 15) "signaling" individuals who encounter women there to remain on their greatest guard.

If anything, "she" hums along, innocuous and lovely only, a harmless and wonderful, kelpy, "precise" part in the machine of the earth.

> she has done it
> and if only I can learn
> every move   each supple turn
> I will do it too (19)

Friesen does not launch into a lyrical reminiscence of love lost and love made possible by the presence of a supple girl. Other than being such a singular love poem and such a lyrical, individualist, courtly prayer for maternity's acceptance of the lonely poet, this poem simply announces that beauty as woman "easily" crosses the fires of hell. She "does it," and he too wishes for the gift to cross through hell with charm, with ease and without the guilt or fear the official "brimstone church" raised him on and which by implication ironically sustains him. He desires rebirth—though he does not directly use this biblicism—and the consequent suppleness enough to walk hell's fire charmed and unharmed. Paradoxically, he has already "done it" in his very coming, in parting the fronds, and in watching woman there. He forgets his ability, apparently, as soon as he succeeds. In actuality, he asks not for an original ability of some sort but for the gift of memory. He wishes for strength to remember the past and let it authenticate and stabilize his present.

> brethren   just for you
> I will walk through hell unsinged
>
> I will be muscle and flame
> and stand where I belong
> my bare feet on fire
> I will be a whirling dervish
> throw glowing cinders on my shoulders (19)

Here the poem ends; but it ends oddly. He suddenly determines to take on the courage of his convictions, and to traverse hell "unsinged" for his, as he has called them in "accomplice," "stiff-necked mennonites," for his brothers. He will cross through hell for the church's sake to defy it, yet he also will cross it for his people's sake in order to show the way across. He will point out for them its harmlessness. He will be the fearless poet who sets the example they need to free them from their bondage to the exacting and joyless, "searing" sun. A fakir crosses burning coals unharmed. Literature sometimes speaks of the poet, too, as a "faker," Plato not the least of those who thought of poets as imitators representing in words what already existed more truly as object. As is commonly known, Plato's hierarchy of authenticity declined in this way: Idea, form, object, spoken word, written word.

The complication of this ending for the poem and poetic explorer, though, lies not in the duplicity of "brethren"; rather, it has to do with the poet's sudden vivacity and nervous restlessness. Instead of moving peacefully and easily as he does at the beginning of the poem when entering hell, or as does the girl he admires with her hypnotic sway and precise step, he promises to become male and "muscular," himself "flaming" as if he burnt with fire, a "whirling dervish" on the fire. The poem pictures a poet in a classical visionary frenzy, precisely in opposition to the sedate picture of the girl who inspires him. He whirls and flexes muscles suspiciously like a young man vainly attempting to impress a young woman of recent acquaintance. She crosses hell with competence; he will cross it with incompetence.

Regardless of his relative competence as the poet against the sun (which is to say, in this case, for hell), whirling and flexing useless biceps in a work that requires maternal patience and calm, "letter to the brimstone church" sets up the distinction between official spirituality and the spirituality the material makes possible. This material spirituality is too frightening for the regular masculine group subject even simply to approach, much less peep at or from which to derive inspiration. This poem's narrative retells the story of Actaeon spying on a naked Diana. Diana in the myth is, of course, a product of official, classical spirituality (Apollonian light, sun light) and unlike the harmless, lithe girl of Friesen's hell. Juno turns poor Actaeon into a deer at Diana's insistence, after which Diana's hounds naturally tear him to pieces. The maternal, the feminine, sexuality in general, suffer terrible onslaughts in classical mythology. Forces pursue and kill all unfilial and unchaste beings. Only the gods ravish women with impunity; then, however, the women they seduce are commonly lower on the scale of cosmic being and so not of sufficient status to have to be treated non-violently. Sex and violence, in other words, go hand in hand in the hierarchically determined relationships of official religion and spirituality. The sun is a "cold cold light," in Friesen's own words (*The Shunning* 39).

The poet, however, presents for us another, more authentic spirituality than official. It is to be recovered in the material, in the earth, not in the sun and that symbol's rejection of the body. Non-images or non-figurative language best represent this embodied, material spirit. I have been arguing, in effect, that the official spiritual and the lyrical poem share common interests, while the material and the non-lyrical poem share a different set of strategies altogether. What Friesen, in "letter to the brimstone church," constructs lyrically with consummate skill in figures and tropes, establishing thereby a great sense of irony in the combination of method and content, he already materially constructs in this book without symbolism or lyrical strategy. Such a material meaning moves in the two poems "closet" and "seeing."

"closet" tells us unforgettably about his father's *active* material life in material terms.

I finger the khaki shirt
he wore on his last working day
before he unbuttoned

along the collar   stain of sweat
faint salt smell of him alive
even as he lies
past mattering in his grave (*bluebottle* 7)

Not entirely material, this poem contains a few metaphoric moments. Very specific to the tension between spirit and matter, they speak to the issue Friesen's aesthetic confronts in the entire book. The poem provides all the information needed, without suggestive restraint or secret plenty: the shirt's colour; the time when father wore it; the crumpledness of much use during a whole working day; the smell and sight of sweat on the collar; and even the less present but still highly physical material and active decay the father's body continues to undergo at the very moment the poet rummages in his closet, "past mattering in the grave" (7). Mostly the images refer the reader to nothing abstract. They describe matter. About life more than death, they tell us of what "matters" materially to those who live.

work pants sharply creased
have fallen from the wooden hanger
I see wrinkles behind the knees
where he stooped or bent

lenses of the eye-glasses
reveal striations
of his eye-lashes on dust

I can't imagine what he saw
as he lay thin and bare
in that dark place (7)

To the extent that Friesen at this point in his writing career recognizes the function of the material, he creates a material poem with all the senses of the reader engaged in seeing what death means, as well as what a father's death means to the son alive to remember the event. The poem, though constructed without excessive literary symbolism, yet makes use of the objective correlative without problematizing it and so the claim must be made that it proceeds by discovering a way of representing the material world and the materiality of writing that incorporates excess and plenty with their obvious inability to be, or unwillingness to attempt to be, exact. The objective correlative in the passage above of the lenses with their striations is a precisely worded image, as precise in words as the girl in hell in "letter to the brimstone church" is precise in her graceful step. Friesen's fiery dancing and "whirling dervish" activity will, with great contrariness of meaning, be less excessive (as whirling dervish implies) than greatly restrained and moderate and, in fact, secretive in affect and effect.

The poem "seeing" shows the same attempt at material writing but with a similar quickness of image, deftness of line and thought, possibly characteristic of a little girl talking of her fear of disappearance, but most likely fitting the poet's sense of how a good imagistic poem might present a specific material content and context:

> when I die
> I'll keep my eyes open
> so I can come back
> she said
> if you see someone
> as high as the chimney
> flying
> it's only Marijke
>
> I'll fly in the rain
> my eyes wide
> seeing all the trees
> herbie my cat
> and the small houses (13)

Doubtless, a child would likely dream of flying, and furthermore think of herself as flying *high* in a flight at the height of the house chimney. This is good verisimilitude. The rain, however, seems rather arbitrary, as if Friesen wished it to represent tears, especially since drops enter the little girl's wide-opened eyes as forces blow her through the falling rain. The apposite myth is that of Icarus, but missing here is the ambition to get to heaven, missing the Apollonian sun-idolatry. I feel quite sure of Friesen's own serious intention to replace the patriarchal figure in the myth with a maternal figure: the generative female principle thrives even after the father and authority dies. He shows us, simultaneously with competent modernist imagery, the simplicity of this maiden, her longing for the ground under her feet and not to fly too near the sun, as well as her sad little attempt to stay here on earth in its warm "hell," so to speak, by grasping the chimney (with all that image's energy gleaned from Blake and "The Chimney Sweep," substituting Blake's boy with a girl), fearing the unknown represented by flying itself. Death in the funeral's aftermath paradoxically makes the little girl wish to fly the earth and to be near to it. Imagistically complex, the poem yet remains material, with few of those sorts of figurative or allusive complexities that require an erudite "initiated" audience. It employs questionable strategies of presentation for a poem that presents a material prairie Mennonite Canadian world instead of the lyrico-symbolic one typical of major literature.

As "seeing" demonstrates, Friesen's poetry in these first four books struggles to present materially a prairie Mennonite Canadian world, but only partially succeeds in ridding itself of the complex lyrical image and its aesthetics based on restraint. Much later in his career, Friesen makes the discovery that long, apparently excessive lines with run-on thoughts (of the sort found more in Di Brandt's poetry) *can* represent the unofficial material world more materially than short, pithy ones, although as I have shown earlier, he inclines toward intense mysticism once he actually begins to use the long line. He seems unable to shake free of the constraints of modernist imagism, despite his consciousness of the power of the material. To do what he does here in "closet," and again with "seeing" a few pages later, is commendably to attempt to construct a voice that speaks for the material prairie but that unfortunately still uses lyrical tools that, in some respects, have never been effective for this country (the persistent short line, the objective image, and others). The material, as quick reflection tells us, is not best presented by strategies of restraint and secrecy, but by those that place the author and his people, his European people, in a vulnerable light, unknowing and fully cooperative with the reigning place that has succoured them. Why is this so? It is so because lyrical, intensely elisive, major writing, deriving from the various literary conventions and social formations of four thousand years of life in that "other" place, tends to leave out the body, to become increasingly "spiritual" and non-material in content, to wish to control the new space by being "frigid" and doling out the body in snippets. It controls through disappointment. It controls through giving a little in return for a lot. Lyrical writing represents the gathered wisdom of the old place and, brought to the new place, rudely insists on its spiritual privilege. Lyrical writing is both fear and control. Material writing is a symptom of vulnerability *before* the body of the new place, before the vitality and fullness of the new place. Write the body and you write the new place. That's why. The material is best presented by strategies of excess, blunder, non-blunder, both lengthy and precise expositions of a complex idea, total exhaustion of possibilities of meanings confidently recorded on the page, non-semantic strategies, pedantic overstatement of the simple, and a general oversupplying of the requirements of the semantic demand, among others. But the poet, and most of the rest of us, too, suffer from a vanity that makes material writing unattractive, since we would rather be recognized and celebrated for our intelligent survey of, our precise mastery of, things. A busy non-secrecy (lyrical training—our training—is all about the secret. It is training to be secretive and requires the audience to be initiated into certain conventions and reading rites of passage) requires an awareness of the nature of the material for which Friesen shows little facility. He constructs his poems either *barely*, without signs of excess when they are very material (by which I mean when they are not clearly cleverly allusive or densely suggestive), or, in his later books, in apparent *excess* with long lines and many words when they are most lyrical.

The discussion so far of the lyrical and the poetic strategies of Friesen's early poems indicates that more than any other element of his work, they problematize the conflict between the major and the minor, between the lyric and the material poem. This purpose is announced in *bluebottle*, it is illustrated in the particular mixture of some solidly lyrical and some solidly material poems, in *the lands i am* and *bluebottle*, and it is most clearly expressed in *The Shunning* and in *Unearthly Horses*.

This knowledge of the conflict between the lyric and the material poem does not surface in *The Shunning* as a main concern. There that conflict is already naturalized. The aesthetic incorporates the struggle, making its metapoetic appearance less necessary. The opposition between the lyric and the material aesthetics functions, in other words, as a fully operative mode in that book. Sometimes the poem is lyrical, sometimes material, according to the thematic and tonal purposes of the poet. Friesen's sense of the strength of the material, minor, politically explicit poem appears nowhere more solidly than in *The Shunning*. This same quiet force of an incorporated aesthetic also modulates *Unearthly Horses,* and much could be said about that book in light of the question of Friesen's poetic (prophetic) Canadian material purpose. For my purposes, however, a closer look at certain parts of *The Shunning* adequately explains Friesen's material/lyrical dynamics.

The Shunning tells the story of the religious shunning and subsequent suicide of Peter Neufeld, a Manitoba farm boy of conservative Mennonite stock. The story is told through the diary entries of Mrs. Hiebert, a midwife, and of Dr. Blanchard, as well as by poems about and in the voices of Peter and Johann Neufeld, Peter's wife Helena, Johann's wives Carolina and Ruth, and Johann's daughter Anna. All their contributions help the reader gradually to piece together what happens to precipitate the shunning, what various church members think of Peter, what they think of the shunning, how Johann relates to his wives and child, the opinions of neighbours and church members on various topics relevant to the shunning, and so on.

> it was july   and the sun
> there was a *tsocka boum* and a rope swing
> Peter sat upright   motionless
> all afternoon he gazed unseeing across his land
> everyone else was inside   Helena   the children
>
> only
>
> two horses   muzzle to muzzle
> stand against the fence   tails flicking flies

> Brummer   hot on the trail   yelping in the trees
>
> and Peter on the swing
>
> that sunday was the first day of his shunning (29)

In this passage, a third of the way through the book, Friesen chooses a simple, unadorned language for the most part. The setting where Peter learns of his shunning is Manitoba Mennonite, considering the use of the Low German name for the Manitoba alder. It is a pioneer Canadian place with animals waving tails and running in the bush. Friesen's readers bake outside in July under a hot sun. There is a tree with a rope swing, on which Peter sits with Mosaic patience, looking unseeing in a reverie out over the farmland. A dog barks and hunts somewhere far away; horses nuzzle each other and stand restless, tails swatting flies.

But tension resides in Eden. Of the members of his family, only Peter sits outside. All the others, inside, look out at him, as if he posed a danger to them, as if he might hurt them, or as if he must not be approached, touched, or loved. And, of course, Peter's exclusion from normal social concourse is the subject of the poems that follow. Peter's shunning means that none of his family or friends may speak to him or interact with him until he admits his sin and repents of it. When he repents, all will be forgiven and he may again be loved and befriended. "For love they will come back," says the old woman Rebecca of the unruly children in Miller's *The Crucible*. Here, in the high religion of Steinbach-area Mennonites, love is a lure, a seduction, a tantalizing impossibility for someone with the convictions and moral certainty of a Peter Neufeld.

Pat Friesen's hero holds strong convictions. Friesen presumably constructs that sort of person as his "ideal man." An individualist *par excellence*, such a man stands up for truth, regardless of the cost to himself. In that sense, this individualist (in the American tradition of Walt Whitman, Daniel Webster, Abe Lincoln, Billy Graham, and so on), imperturbable to death, devout and loyal, Peter epitomizes the good churchman, much more of a convincing religious figure than the milksops who come to read him his rights.

There are mosquitoes on Loewen's hands one on his cheek
but he pages on and reads.

It is a fearful thing to fall into the hands of the living God.

Bible closes. They bow their heads and Loewen prays for
my salvation and that they will do the right thing. I move
toward Loewen as he prays. He backs down. Funk and Penner
stumble off the porch. Loewen shuffles aside as I go down and
walk to the barn. (28)

Friesen upholds truth. He upholds the artistic presentation of
the truth about the violent hypocrisy of the church. This truth-
concern expresses itself thematically above in the "mosquito-slap-
ping" scene with its "tiny scarlet splash there and a wreckage of
black legs and wings" (28) —figuratively the death these church-
men cause with their shunning, and the violence to Peter's relatives inflicted by their rectitude and paranoid exertion of the ban
of silence and separation goes almost unnoticed by these men.
See how delicate the image? How gentle and lovely the creature
violated? How lyrical and outside real experience? Wings suggest
heaven and grace; legs, black and broken, present the fragile
body tangled in sudden death, the human body, that short-lived
entity whose legs carry it around in a too quickly finished and
busy life. The word "legs" always contains something of sex in all
English literature (Toby Belch: "Taste your legs" [*Twelfth Night*
III.i.87]). But more than theme and its imagistic development,
Friesen's desire to *think* the church and the Mennonite community (rather than to receive its teachings already full blown)
shows up in numerous qualities that may be called minor.

Friesen's simple, unadorned language in this poetic narrative
tells non-lyrically about something very much of this land; a
shunning differs "here" from one somewhere else, distinct in
Canada from a shunning in the Old World. Here it is not to be
captured by the prescriptive responses sought for and achieved by
thick lyrical layers. Here a shunning (or poetry, the two are inter-
changeable) is letting yourself think, the way Thom, in *Peace
Shall Destroy Many,* thinks against his parents and his "community's" non-thinking acceptance of old beliefs that others had
thought for him before and so should be adequate as knowledge.

But, in exactly the way that such received biblical wisdom thinks poorly, motivated by a fear of change, so the lyrical presentation of Peter Neufeld's shunning would be a not-thinking-very-well the facts of shunning here on the prairies of Canada. The lyrical presentation would derive from fear of hard (facile, bland, material) thought about it that itself derives from surplus and from having no established moral structures easily and effectively standing between the event and the subject. "Nothing works" is not a cry of despair, but a statement about reality and its flows. The phrase "no structures work" simply explains what Peter experiences in his long insistence against the church, against Old World prescriptions. The poems establish that the church frequently asked Peter to recant his belief in the impossibility of hell. The church inflicts the punishment of shunning when Peter's adamant stubbornness finally drives them to it.

That very real "nothing works" is Peter's pacing in the fields and in the woods in the wilderness behind his farmyard, as witnessed by Anne, Johann's daughter.

> Uncle Peter left people alone and he wanted to be left alone. He would go into the bush when he felt too strong about one thing or another. Like when he was angry. And you never saw a temper like his . . . . I sometimes sneaked up on him near Buffalo Field . . . . Anyways, usually he was quiet. One time, though, he was swearing and punching a poplar tree with his fist. When I went to look at the tree after he had gone, there was blood smeared on the bark. I wouldn't have wanted to see his knuckles. (22-23)

The real "nothing works" is also Peter's sitting and watching from the swing, a watching that ends in his "real" death, too, at the end of his real (multiple) gun.

> the crouped child choking
> and mother holding him over a steaming kettle
>
> the child sprawled on gravel   licking his blood
>
> the child   rolling his pantlegs to the knees
> wading down twin creek   cattails bowing
> this boy   his feet and calves mud-smeared
> is man here   the caught corpse

one hand in water
one boot off   the other untied
his white foot nudging the rifle stock

his temple   a blue hole the bullet made (48)

This is the book's hinge poem; everything Friesen attempts in his poetic theorizing of the material/lyrical depends on "material" success here. Just at the point when Peter's death by his own hand is visualized, the poet needs to show distancing from "symbolic reterritorialization" and invent the world of death with a bodily, fulsome, poor, intensity of language.

I find in this poem a combination of empirical "addition" of details and "symbolic reterritorialization" of the sort Deleuze and Guattari describe in their definition of minor literature. They speak of Kafka's "minor" writing as material and rich, not with symbolism but with "material intensities," inventive, non-signifying, and "poor" in the lyrical conventions (symbols).

> Well, one can go even farther; one can push this movement of deterritorialization of expression even farther. But there are only two ways to do this. One way is to artificially enrich this German, to swell it up through all the resources of symbolism, of oneirism, of esoteric sense, of a hidden signifier. This is the approach of the Prague School, Gustav Meyrink and many others, including Max Brod. But this attempt implies a desperate attempt at symbolic reterritorialization, based in archetypes, Kabbala, and alchemy, that accentuates its break from the people and will find its political result only in Zionism and such things as the "dream of Zion." Kafka will quickly choose the other way, or, rather, he will invent another way. He will opt for the German language of Prague as it is and in its very poverty. Go always farther in the direction of deterritorialization, to the point of sobriety. Since the language is arid, make it vibrate with a new intensity. Oppose a purely intensive use of language to all symbolic or even significant or simply signifying usages of it. Arrive at a perfect and unformed expression, a materially intense expression. (*Toward a Minor Literature* 19)

Friesen's language in this poem is at once ascetic (poor, sober) and signifying (logical), so it does not, in the definition of the most effective minor literature, "arrive at a perfect and unformed expression, a materially intense expression." A form of "addition" of details does occur, but missing the "ands" and "buts," for one thing. Such a piling on of details without signifying expression would be a form of "poor" language, of the language of intensities, making no use of signification or tradition of signification, but only of materiality (feelings, rich vibrancy of excitation, busy interaction with surrounding objects/bodies): affects without specific causes or effects. In his *Dialogues*, Deleuze equates empiricism with materiality, represented in grammar by conjunctions and not by subjects and objects. In sentence structure, in other words, empiricism (materiality) is best represented by the run-on sentence. Such empirical writing would be, in Deleuze's thinking, symbolically "poor" writing. In Friesen's poem, we get contradictory writing: we get not the empirical, conjunctive "addition," or "poverty," but a form of addition in which silences replace conjunctions; silences form the transitions. The poem's "sentences" simultaneously give intensity and take it away. In the end, they proceed by the richness of silence, of symbolic reterritorialization, by the strategies of lyric restraint.

Silences, secretive, authorial and dominating as they are, are suspect of high purpose, of the transcendental signifier. The economy of the alliteration and consonance of "calves . . . caught corpse" speaks of an uneasiness about poverty of language (intensities), alliteration being a principal lyrical convention, propped up by and propping up official moral structures. The alliteration, in its restraint, its elision, its economy of expression, indicates uneasiness about resisting morality at such a raw moment, at the moment of death, morality offering, as it does, only one possible reading of death and of the moment of death. The stylistic dying—not unlike the reclining of Bernini's ecstatic St. Teresa— with one hand in the water, and one boot off, derives its power from the classical dichotomy of unity within disunity: the one foot is booted (dressed, prepared, orderly), the other *was* booted (undone, changed, disordered, vulnerable); one hand is in water (female, drowned, growing, wet, corruptible), the other is in air (male, breath, thoughtful/intellectual, aspiring, ageless). The stylistic dying points still, even here in this undoing of Peter Neufeld of what we assume to be the Steinbach area, up to a divine order that remains beyond our understanding but that nevertheless somehow exists, and which traditional poesy helps to recall and signify. Earth, in classical poetry, stands for what is fallen, corrupt, material, gross, heavy, low, witless, stupid and unspiritual. Earth (water) stands for what no refined man or woman would wish for or strive to be like. Heaven, however, better signified by the air, near God, high, perfect in its motions, incorruptible, eternal, unchanging, spiritual, and privileged, represents in classical poetry that toward which thinking mankind aspires. Friesen's dichotomies in this hinge poem suggest the classical thought of the old (Old World), not the materiality of newness and invention. Friesen orders the cattails to "bow" to this boy, to this "saviour," this divine man who gives his life to thinking against evil and conformity, who in death dies for his community. This sense of worship due Peter Neufeld for his Messianic dying continues in the classic contrast between white and black ("his white foot") and even more precisely and evocatively in the making of his body a "temple" ("his temple a blue hole the bullet made"), a biblical allusion to 1 Corinthians 3:16 and 2 Corinthians 6:16. One traditionally worships, if one is Christian, the whiteness of angels, of God, of all heavenly things, which never, biblically, show up coloured black. One also worships and reveres the foot of Christ, which, nailed and tortured like the crown of His head, bleeds till it is the purest white (in Christian imaginations). The foot, too, stands for humility and love (in the washing of the feet by true disciples). Much more in the Bible tells us of the worship-training centred on whiteness and feet. The rifle and bullet indicate further that classical dichotomies order this poem, which in so many respects seems to be a simple, clear and local "Canadian" poem. The violence of the rifle and the bullet contrasts to the peace which Christ's life exemplified. Friesen appeals everywhere to the power of the symbolic through contrast and dichotomization: rifle or violence/Christ and peace, mother/father, child/adult, man/woman, earth/sky, earth/blood, feet/head (with particularly high Messianic connections: Psalm 22:16, John 12:3, John 13:5, Romans 16:20), and others. What appears at first to be just a poem about a Canadian boy grown up and dead now by the creek where he once played, turns out instead to be thickly coded lyrically. At critical moral moments and dramatic moments (often the same thing) Friesen turns to convention, to the familiarity of the lyric, either to give his piece punch or because he himself feels uncomfortable with the material when the thinking gets rough. We back away from the void and wish to give it meaning, even if it is the void itself that we take for our meaning.

Contrast the bland and "Canadian," or possibly "prairie" (by which I mean non-conventional) way he describes Dr. Blanchard's activities on the morning of his discovery of Peter Neufeld's suicide. First, an offhand reference to the death: "I'm puzzled by this suicide. I imagine it had something to do with his trouble with the church. Though what that trouble was I don't rightly understand. Strange people" (49). The line lengths happen without significance, the descriptive adjectives happen for no effect but the most common, and the speculations about the central theme/plot of the poem (Peter's death) simply occur without charging the reader emotionally. The journal entry form of this text additionally strengthens the "empirical" quality of the poetry with its necessary easygoing confessional discourse, and its willingness to name the emotions felt by Blanchard. He felt "puzzled"; he "found" strawberries; he "had to go" because of the mosquitoes. We have here the material; we find none of the figuratively charged language readers of the lyric and the epic involuntarily associate with the climactic, lyrical, death scene. Blanchard's account acts as the non-lyrical version of the conventional, highly lyricized, death poem. Coming side by side as they do, these two poems seem almost intentionally to illustrate the two ways of writing poetry.

Other poems also demonstrate Friesen's tendency to go lyrical (non-thinking) at important, emotional moments. Johann's (or what appears to be Johann's) lament/elegy for his dead brother serves as an example.

> now his narrow home
> a mound   a stone
>
> wild rose bushes
> barbed wire
> and headstones on the other side (52)

Notice the markers of the transcendental that we associate with traditional poetry, such as, for instance, mediaeval romantic ballads: the grave equals a "narrow home"; "wild rose bushes" assemble among the images (as in the ballad of "The Three Maries," and "I Have a Young Sister"), telling of forlorn and wasted or unrequited love; barbed wire suggests the indignity of war, an image popular in the humanist poetry of the world wars, in a humanist tradition at least as old as the beginnings of the European Renaissance.

Other examples of the lyrical shortcut in *The Shunning* include the poem describing a darkly brazen and flayed-feeling Sunday after Peter's death, a woman walking home after church.

> Or this.
>
> a woman walking home from church
> her shawl loosens and slips to her shoulders
> she pauses   removes combs and pins
> lifts her face to the sky and shakes out her fiery hair
>
> behind her the sun and golden withers
> of a horse reaching for grass
> beneath the bottom strand of barbed wire
>
> a horse   the sun
> and almost everyone shielding their eyes
>
> on a sunday (58)

The "barbed wire" image connects Johann's lament with this random erotic piece, joining the brothers in ways other than blood. "A woman" provides secrecy, the mystery of no particular woman but one important enough to have a full poem devoted to her. "Fiery hair" and the whole description of the loosening of the body and the clothes mean an abandonment of the restrictions on the erotic that the church enforces. "The sun and golden withers" connote Sunday's holy horses of the apocalypse, the pagan Helios or God's great seeing eye; "golden fleece," we almost say, and all that epic apparatus and quaint emotion and convention from which the lyric derives its themes, methods, and power.

We get from Friesen here the sparse lyrical detail of a modernist poem, like something by Carlos Williams or H.D., the entire image in true imagist concentration of power on the singular experience, the immediate experience, focussed on the poem's last word. It is an admirable imagist poem. You can just imagine the poet putting all his body's weight, almost, behind the pen till it grinds down finally as the poem closes on "sunday." Always in Friesen's lyrics a message, a great theme and humanist truth to be hammered home and gotten across. Always a tragic death, an evil Sunday, a brooding brother like, or only slightly different from, a Cain. Always the hated church but still the church. The lyric has these moments all ready for us. We are its receptacle. We have little to say about it, being readers who are well-trained, well-drilled, made to feel uncomfortable with the comfortable (which is to say, by the uncanny: the "uncomfortable comfortable" is a precise definition of Freud's *unheimlich*— easy scares, horror chambers that frighten but only within endurance because we know we are safe). In other words, the lyric is the official. The official always thinks (via non-thinking) it delivers what it considers the difficult when it delivers the pre-determined and the inane. The lyric and the official are the undangerous.

And in the very next poem, which is largely material and unconventional, the reader still gets the highly elliptical description of the sexual female body, an ellipsis explainable by the long willingness of lyrical literature (Old World serious poetry) to stop in modesty at the threshold or inference of pleasure and love-making (for lack of a better word) or love, unlike, say, Sade's or Rabelais's works.

No Old World lyrical restraint conspires here: no teachings of guilt; no established thinking to keep the subject subjected to the group and to thwart his desires. As Thom in *Peace Shall Destroy Many* reterritorializes his community by thinking against the received wisdom of "by the sweat of your brow," so Patrick Friesen's "watching from the swing" poem and its structural, non-lyrical complacency to the coming death, allow us to *think* the shunning here on the prairies. Not only the shunning we are let to think, but everything. Nothing. We are allowed by the non-moral, non-repressive, non-complexly already structured and imaged and filled and heavily layered poem to think our own minor poem. This thinking the minor poem of death is not an emptiness in the sense of the "nothing there" but an emptiness (if it is an emptiness) of the everything there, the surplus, the multiple, waiting for us to write "the emptiness" of death as we wish. That is, of course, it is *waiting* for us to write it out of power. We are "empowered" by this waiting, it might be said, if that was not a favourite (and fascist) expression of the cause-fighting groups. The poem is a waiting, before the splendid emptiness of the non-structured, the not-already-determined. This waiting is a minor waiting that refuses the major, both thematically and stylistically. The waiting Peter refuses the precepts of the church as profoundly as the waiting ordinary thought of this poem revolts against the endless expectations and cautions and predeterminations that constitute the lyrical style. The moment the poet employs the lyrical style (old conventions of expression, imagery, literary symbolism, rhythm, and much more) the writer/reader jumps to attention and returns to the harness of pulling, pulling his weight. He returns, in other words, to guilt and fear instead of into thinking for himself.

5.

Father, Mother and Mennonite Me:
Di Brandt and the Overthrow of the Mother

Next to Pat Friesen, Di Brandt stands as the second most well-known and influential poet of Mennonite Canada with four books of poetry, a critical text, and a collection of essays. Her concern is most clearly about the fate of women in the world, and specifically women in Mennonite Canadian society. As a way of analyzing the state of the female under patriarchy, she examines her own past and present in an autobiographical style.

The new awareness of the special importance of birth mothers in the world provides cause, Brandt says, for celebration.

> I wish to celebrate in my study the presence of the maternal reproductive body in history, in narrative, and in language, and honour women's reproductive labour in childbirth and childrearing, without which, after all, none of us would be alive. (*Wild Mother Dancing* 10)

In the poetry she wrote after the problem of the missing birth mother in literature became important to her (7), Brandt practises what she preaches. She undertakes to write what few attempt, or at least not with such persistence. She writes the birth mother's subjectivity. She writes this birth mother, directly often, and sometimes indirectly, into each poem and each piece of prose. Feminism and feminist writing provide the theory, the subject, and forum for her raising up to a long-awaited proper place the image of the birth mother in Western texts:

> how long i've listened
> to your cry
>
> in my flesh, singing
> me home.
>
> & now i am fully
> born. i dance
>
> as the trees dance,
> deep-rooted
>
> & rustling in wind.
> my arms caress
>
> air, my mouth fills
> with pleasure,
>
> knowing the earth
> deeply, recognizing
>
> myself in you,
> perfumed, & trembling,
>
> without fear. (*mother, not mother* 75)

This rebirth, a nascent, delicious birth for mother and baby, fills the mother with a new joy and pleasure; as if for the first time she recognizes her place, her identity in the baby she makes. She now, for once, feels fearless. Males and their violence (see all of *Jerusalem, beloved*), textual and physical both, no longer contain nor decentre her now, "fully born" as she finally is.

Brandt claims that essential meaning belongs to females because of their ability to mother, to birth and care for a child whom a mother "gardens" and grows within her biological body. Males lack something. Essentially underprivileged, they attempt the following: appropriate female meaning; avenge themselves for the absence of female meaning within themselves; slaughter and hurt others in a thousand different ways as a general expression of anguish at their alienation from meaning. Underprivileged, to be pitied, and generally inept and violent, they further lack those astonishing and commendable female emotions of love, longing, desire, and joy. These voluptuous emotions derive from and equate with the earth. "Earth" includes, oddly, such ancient cities as Jerusalem, female products of the earth. She writes of Jerusalem:

> . . . i want to be wild &
> unworded, like the wind, blowing through the bare
> branches, toward open sky, i want to learn to fly,
> not with Air Canada, with my own wings, arms
> branching, feathering out, the sea down below,
> roads & houses disappearing, the air sharp & clear,
> Jerusalem rising from her desert bed to meet me
> (*Jerusalem, beloved* 58)

The desire to fly, but not to fly too high in Icarus fashion, already occurs in Pat Friesen's poem "chimney," with the little girl holding onto the house chimney to keep from blowing away after her grandfather dies. The desire for low flight, controlled flight that makes the earth, rather than heaven and divine spirits, the focus of its exhilarated discoveries, expresses itself in the imagined whirling through shops and streets of a *female* city.

> Jerusalem rising from her desert bed to meet me,
> glistening, luminous, her thousand musicians
> playing love songs, the war over, all over, my
> feathered hands caressing her stone hips & thighs,
> her doorways opening to the fragrance of wine,
> olives, feasting, the sky holding us lightly,
> swooning, among clouds (58)

Flying poet, and rising city—erect and growing more erect, in the ways that females grow erect (see Donne's wonderful use of this paradox in "Valediction: Forbidding Mourning")—meet in the sky among the clouds like lovers, the "doorways opening" with their wine fragrance a coy metaphor for female sexuality. The war over, the female city lifts from its "desert bed," where it presumably lay in torpor, into the sky (domain of male spiritual inscription) and joins this other female in busy, freed, now unafraid female desire for the female. The male other, the "fighting men" of Jerusalem (71), hides unseen, his duty done in having fought and ended fighting. The sky, no longer heavy home of the gods, holds Jerusalem and the poet "lightly." The two lovers, poet and female city, occupy with rejoicing what once they might not gambol in. They frolic in the presence of, almost in flirtatious indifference to, an emasculated sky, which holds them lightly up (tenderly, or facilely, or simply indifferent to women now with the end of heroism and war, only taking them lightly, taking their jubilant lesbian sexuality lightly).

Males in Brandt's work, in contrast to females, wish not to succour, but to slaughter and vent their anger in violences of various sorts. The opening section of *Jerusalem, beloved* provides a long series of dramatic approximations of this generality. The persona's emotions on first seeing Israel and Jerusalem resemble those she feels against women who, having birthed children, still resist letting themselves love. *Mother, not mother* poignantly recounts the autobiographical past of the persona's relationship with a mother who, either for personal, religious reasons, or because of the dominance of "the name of the father" over the female spirit, never expressed her love for her daughter. She failed, in other words, to train the daughter to love her own beauty and "womb power" (in contrast to the poet who successfully loves and educates her daughters in the arts of self-love) and so she alienated one whom nature herself attempts to protect from such abandonment.

The logics in *mother, not mother* present the reader with the story of the deterritorialized mother. The poet-persona attempts to come to terms with her feelings for her mother and the causes for her alienation, both from her birth mother and from meaning generally. Foremost, the protagonist of these poems feels ambiguity about motherhood. Motherhood consists not simply of a wonderful state to be cherished, but often a burdensome and thankless one. Why should it always fall to mothers to provide tenderness and sympathy for the world?

why she can't write *the mother,*
though she has birthed two children,

spends half her day feeding clothing
sheltering them,

picking up dirty rolled up socks
cooking macaroni,

though she has stretched herself thin,
scarred skin over bloated belly,

watched leftover blood shoot clotted
like fists from her emptied womb,

though she's exhausted herself, black
& blue, many times

mothering the goddamn fucking world

why she can't write herself around
that,

why she can't put down simply,
i am the mother,

& leave it like that (9)

She cannot simply be the mother, since the performance of an
important set of duties, concerning the state of the entire world
and its beings, waits on her. These supra-maternal duties mean
another sacrifice beyond the sacrifices typically endured by
mothers. In the untitled poem beginning "blackbirds," the poet
provides the reader with a stunning portrait in little, of the universe, as she understands it. The universe, first of all, brims with
colourful, beautiful life: "blackbirds, green ash, purple / fire-
weed" (10). In the midst of this abundance, however, sorrow sits:
"by the river she sat down & wept." In Eden, betrayed and lost,
pain suppresses the joy once offered by abundance and beauty.
The unnamed river indicates primacy, a great, mythic river, possibly the Euphrates, in keeping with the Eden metaphor.
Someone—"she"—sat down once upon a time (later the poem
turns to present tense), and wept. The poet, in Jerusalem, with a

lover (probably nature herself) who consoles her, recalls how she
herself over the years wept more than may be borne by memory:

> the rivers of tears i have cried, an ocean, not
> enough salt water to wash out this cave, this
> temple, this holy place, where you have come,
> visitor, bearing gifts (*Jerusalem, beloved* 42)

"She," the unnamed subject in "blackbirds," takes on herself the
entire burden of our mythic forebears who, cast out time and again
from their homeland, wander in painful insecurity through wilder-
nesses, time and again winding up as slaves serving the unknown
gods of their foreign masters. "She" takes on this weight of suffering, this history, in the particular wording of her action, which
echoes the biblical account of Israelite oppression:

> By the rivers of Babylon,
> there we sat down, yea, we
> wept, when we remembered
> Zion (Psalm 137, 1)

The female gender of the weeping one provokes the connection
with the story of Eve, a story significant for Brandt's purposes
because essentially elided and overshadowed by that of Adam.
What history records of mankind's doings over the last four
thousand years, history records mostly about and through male
experience. "She" represents Eve's experience instead (here and in
other of Brandt's books); the subject of this story will be female.
Females will be given their due subjectivity:

> While I do not wish to valorize maternal experience or mater-
> nal narrative at the expense of other subject positions, therefore,
> I do wish to argue for a politicized reading of maternal narra-
> tive that takes into account the mother's traditional absence
> and the reasons for it, a politicized reading act that is *on the
> side* of maternal subjectivity. (*Wild Mother Dancing* 9-10)

Female subjectivity will be honoured here in "blackbirds," but in
what way? Will this consist only of a story of endless suffering? On
the contrary, despite her sorrowful alienation, friendship exists for
her: "the weeds keeping her company, / when he would not" (10).

Earth and nature gather around her when she, the poem's subject, feels bereft. Weeds, usually vilified in literature, here come to her as friends. Those with great suffering in their past appreciate small goodnesses. Moreover, in Brandt's work the earth stands for that loving mother of life whom human children forget to love in return, as in this passage from *questions i asked my mother*:

> hear them whispering mother my unborn
> children crying their sorrow without a
> name why don't you love me why am i bad
> how will i ever hold them all i need a
> dozen arms a hundred breasts i need a
> thousand love songs mother a lap as big
> as earth (58)

Loved children, cocky and self-centred, forget to love their birth mothers (see *Jerusalem, beloved* 64). Regularly, in moments of greatest pain or exuberance, the female subjects of Brandt's texts rediscover meaning, friendship, and love in the nurturing earth, which feels a common bond with its female offspring (see *Wild Mother Dancing* 16-17). The earth loves her "when he would not."

> because the trees outside your window are
> splendid, the wind in the branches waves the sky
> along, grandly. because the earth under your feet is
> there, every morning, solid, profound, hanging in
> air, filled with gravity & lightness, keeping you there
> . . . .
> . . . this earth is my home, my body, my mother,
> unafraid & so, unutterably, beautiful (*Jerusalem, beloved* 32)

Males in Brandt's universe contend with females instead of supporting them in their difficult task of mothering. Alienated from and jealous of female (and earth's) procreative power, males wage war against the partners with whom they might instead mutually labour to provide loving care. The abandonment of females by the "he" of this poem represents the actions of men in Brandt's poetry generally.

The sky, classically male and indifferent to human needs,

only *seems* benign and friendly to the weeping woman (recall Friesen's similar perception of the friendlessness of sky and sun): "the sky sometimes a delicate pink / like the petals of the roses" (*mother, not mother* 10). Where human men abandon their women, the masculine sky in Brandt's poetry acts "lightly." Sky loves earth in this world of prelapsarian nature and fallen humankind.

> a great circle, coming round, like the sky, its
> long arm reaching across, east to west, your
> life coming back to meet you, greet you, in
> flashes, green, yellow, pink, against the night
> (*Jerusalem, beloved* 66)

It seems to me that Brandt wishes to show her readers the wonder that, in a world that humans endlessly violate, there exists, if we only possessed the wisdom and will to see it, a still lovely, loving, nurturing natural world.

> the river's green today,
> like the leaves over my head,
>
> so vivid this time of year,
> just before they turn colour.
>
> everything's singing,
> do you hear it in the wind?
>
> the whole world's in orgasm
> this late summer day
>
> every tree spreading its
> legs to the sky,
>
> a hundred dark crotches
> on every trunk, (*mother, not mother* 63)

We destroy a nature that would love us and teach us how to love it, if we only chose to accommodate it. "She," the female poet in tune with her female-loving universe (*Jerusalem, beloved* 47), shows us the means of its accomplishment.

a billion leaves shudder

their ancient, secret
vegetable delight.

i'm lying here, my sore
back pressed against grass,

against the earth, all eyes,
all ears, all nose,

listening, watching, smelling
the gorgeous world,

every pore a vagina,
every sound, every green

shade of leaf & tree
a lover (*mother, not mother* 63-64)

Brandt's narrator frequently stands or lies down among trees (see the opening poem of *Agnes in the sky*, for instance), which she nurtures and protects in order herself to receive loving protection from them. Her love for herself, people and nature tends these word trees.

you come bearing gifts green apples
glistening in a red bowl you have
waited all your life for this moment
tended your small tree carefully (*Agnes in the sky* 19)

Father-violence, mother-fear, and a mass of related "exquisite" hurts threaten her little inner tree of life: "weathered high winds listened to / the world's pain each delicate / exquisite hurt you have wept" (19). Possibly most precisely, this little tree represents the child within her, who, the poet imagines, never properly came to birth, her unborn self. In other words, the poetic narrator makes love to herself here in "the river's green today" (*mother, not mother* 63). The reader accommodates her self-love because she attempts with sincerity to describe a world still uneducated in the art of loving women or the strength they represent, the strength and wonder of generation. Dramatically loving herself

here in "the taste of earth," the poet practises the textual maternal subjectivity to which she vowed to devote her words.

The universe as the poet creates it so far in "blackbirds"
includes such archetypes as an abundant world, a river by which
a woman weeps, and a sky coloured in gentle pink like rose
petals. Now she brings into play the next type: children related
to. The fallen world as Brandt imagines it treats children badly.

> the children banging their bicycle
> locks against the bridge railing,
>
> their extraordinary carnival of
> grief, in the night, (*mother, not mother* 10)

Our children live traumatized, loveless, and abandoned lives.
The noise of bikes "banging" against metal railings simply stands
in place of all the "carnival" of weeping, wailing, pleading of the
world. Grief pours out of the children:

> against the dying universe, against
> absent mothers
>
> against the failure of fathers. (10)

Like the suffering of children, the dying of the universe finds frequent expression in Brandt's work, suggested, for instance, by the
words "munitions factory" (*Jerusalem, beloved* 31).

Virtually all instances of violence in *mother, not mother* and
Jerusalem occur in association with a male figure. Female figures
represent peace and love, or at worst, the absence of a love they
would naturally give, were it not for the way patriarchy con-
quered, humbled, mistreated, and silenced women.

> needing to be
> touched.
>
> my back is full
> of terror still,
>
> remembering
> the hand,

the belt across
my spine,

the hole between
my shoulder blades,

where i quiver
& taste dirt (28)

The perpetrator of abuse against this child must be a father, given the associations with which the rest of Brandt's poems leave us. The non-particularized belt-wielder leads the reader to understand a universal hitting father, or if not a father, then at least an angry, authoritative male. The child who is hit, since it too receives no name, becomes the generalized female child within, powerless to be freed or born until the victim confronts the violator. Memory stays infantile, fixed not on a flux of things, not focussed on the movement of events, but on a single and fierce image of the hitting hand. Not only the memory and consciousness remember, the very body of this woman carries the ever present and determining "terror" about with her. There is no forgetting, then, when the mind and the body independently hold and bind and contain the former violence, static and hegemonic, in a relentless remembering. Theorists know very well of this quality of silence, as the way memory manages not to forget. David Carroll, in his introduction to Jean François Lyotard's *Heidegger and "the jews,"* describes the silence of holocaust survivors in similar terms. They refuse to speak of the endless killing inflicted on them because speaking would lessen it and let off the perpetrators and history with too little punishment and too much of the crime "forgotten" by the telling itself.

Regardless of the passive hold on her of the memory of the "hand seared into flesh," another force eventually frees her body from its mnemonic catatonia.

you touch my
forehead,

my left shoulder,
where i am

broken-winged,
you say, & healing.

you touch my body
& i am held

like a sea, fronds
waving in slow

motion, waves
lapping shore.

the sun in our
faces,

dazzling. (28-29)

A woman, "Joan Turner," to whom the poem dedicates itself, touches her "body" and she feels new love: "& i am held." The victim is an angel, "broken-winged." The implication here is, How can someone hurt and control another human who represents innocence, goodness, love, joy, pleasure, friendship and intelligence? How can someone punish and break the wings of that which is good and wholesome (remember the brother who swings cats by their tails in *questions i asked my mother*)? Why would an innocent woman be so terrorized? By way of answer, love from another woman's touch begins to heal the persona. With the touch of love, dramatic movement begins: "held // like a sea, fronds / waving in slow // motion," and "waves / lapping shore." (See Friesen's previous use of "frond.") The sun radiates in their faces, not in hers alone: a social bond forges itself in this movement from what once was pain and incommunicability.

In brief, males commit violence. Females bear the brunt of that violence and, made passive by it, find release only when they eventually speak out and join forces against their imprisonment in its painful memory. Women are victims, males are perpetrators. Mennonite language perpetuates female silence and aggressive male authority:

the body remembers being
beaten & tortured & killed.

i stole the language
of their kings & queens,

but i didn't bow down to it,
i didn't become a citizen.

how hard it is to tell a story
so it can be heard

how easily the reader climbs
on top of it,

pronouncing judgement, (30)

Friesen, too, speaks of "kings" in a similar vein, if you recall. The memory of violence "the body carries . . . well hidden" fears speaking, speaks slowly and methodically, like a child learning to articulate basic sounds, and as if the first sound this child-adult learned to make is a loud cry for mother:

MMMMMMMMMMMMMMM
AAAAAAAAAAAAAAAAAAAAAA
MMMMMMMMMMMMMMM
EEEEEEEEEEEEEEEEEEEEEEEE (31)

How much the narrator needed her mother "through the centuries." She finds just such love later in her travels in her meeting with the female revolutionaries and Bacchantes in *Jerusalem, beloved* on her tour of the holy lands, as if she has travelled the world specifically in search of maternal care and compassion. Even the city of Jerusalem becomes her maternal lover in one of these later poems (*Jerusalem, beloved* 58). Having travelled in search of maternal love, she finds it eventually after this "Joan" sets her free by her touch. (Recall Patrick Friesen's own brilliant pursuit of "touch" in this land as opposed to spirituality in that land. It becomes increasingly clear to me that these two poets build their aesthetics upon each other's works.) At this point in the book, the mother still remains an absent mother and the child within the poet still unborn. Feminism tells males (and humans generally) a truth about the violated female, if males could only listen well enough and begin to express regret and contrition.

poem for a guy who's
thought about feminism

& is troubled by it,
but not enough:

what you don't want
to know can hurt you,

& will, perhaps even
kill you, as it has killed

so many others, women,
whales, birds, Indians,

Jews, even the golden-
haired sons of men,

the privileged ones,
the chosen (48)

Though feminism teaches all mankind that a terrible litany of killings must some day be redeemed by the death of the male, the narrator frequently feels too weak to speak about it.

i long again
for the old pain,

the fist in the face,
the twisted twirly

fate, the bitter taste
of absence

on the tongue, you.

i admit i have cried
at night for my father

& his Word,
the old terrible God. (52)

A loneliness drives the feminism of this narrator at times to weaken into a state of longing for the very paternal pain and oppression against which she has pitted her intelligence. This "Word," this "terrible God," this "garbage," this maleness, gives way to the steady growth of the "earth pushing" and "flesh singing" (52) within her, however, and for these teleological reasons she succumbs only temporarily to the temptation to find familiar belonging within the old hierarchy, and easy understanding within "the Old Story" (53).

The strength of the female to endure despite the tyranny of the patriarchal "Old Story" finds quaint expression in a shamanistic account of a second birth. As always, Brandt makes use of the types of the "Old Story," in this case imagining her release from the static power of the name of the father through a Christlike rebirth: the story of the birth of Christ as a child, much like this one of the narrator's birth, begins first with the account of a child's birth into the world.

The poet describes the birth of her inner child. This poem does double duty, ostensibly describing the birth of the child, which she so proudly carries in one of the first poems in the book (16), but more dramatically presenting the birth of the inner child, which male violence "over the centuries" imprisoned within her: "how you pushed your way / fiercely, between her thighs" (59). The mother here sees herself from a distance; the child forces its way out between "her" thighs. A disconnection characterizes the immediate mother-child relationship, one that the poet laments throughout her works as existing between herself and her own mother. This disconnection, however, is only a waiting, a fearfulness lest she will not be able to love her girl child as she feels she has been unloved by her mother. Since this girl child is her inner child as much as her "real," biological child, the waiting represents decades of expectation for something to be born that has lived in a sort of eternal gestation within. The touch of the woman in the poem dedicated to Joan Turner brings about this new, awaited movement in the mental womb: waiting for Messiah; waiting for Godot; waiting for woman's emergence. The waiting stands for the long silence that she and women generally have endured. At long last the baby emerges and instantly the infant becomes the adult, carrying the mother on her back.

> & now you carry her
> so strangely, on your back,
>
> into the evening,
> her old bones glinting,
>
> eyes glowing into the dark.
> the reversals in everything.
>
> the distance between cells
> dividing & dividing (59)

Where the narrator thought all was lost, now all twists into possibility with the birth of the inner/outer child. Where maternity appears impossibly bound and caught, it frees itself in the simple division of cells.

That child-saviour speaks in the poetry it writes to force an accounting from violence. In a poem that tells of the contrariness of the outer child who "wouldn't come along / i couldn't make you" (70), the newborn inner child calms the maternal screaming with its political wisdom.

> just stop once in a while
> in your screaming
>
> & listen, your armoured
> anger against bombs
>
> & pollution & plastic,
> against me:
>
> there is holiness
> in everything,
>
> even our fear
> haunting us at night
>
> wants to be loved (70)

In the untitled poem beginning "in this version," the violence the speaker resents is, however, also a temptation. She "falls in love // with the dragon" (71) hoping that if she "loves him enough" he will "stop breathing fire on her skin" and "be a man"

(71). She gets to know "him" by loving him and "swallow[ing] his come" (71). Now, seeded with this violence, in need of new strength, new ability to resist the dragon, she turns to nature, to its light, its wind sounds. Learning from her, she slowly "grows / a new tongue, // to sing (screaming" (73).

The words and speaking the poet learns from nature, together with her long apprenticeship in the bedroom of the dragon, allow her finally to "sing screaming." Till recently she has been complicit in dragon violence through her silence (and again, I hear echoes of Patrick Friesen, and his use of "accomplice"). She sings now of the terrible stranger who haunts her dreams.

> sometimes,
> in the middle of the night,
>
> there he is again,
> my dark haired
>
> dark eyed bogey man,
> my monster,
>
> my stranger. (76)

Freud speaks of "strangers . . . felling your woods" as the emblem of the uncanny (*Art and Literature* 342-43). This Freudian, uncanny figure stalks her memory. Before his memory she faints, powerless. Earlier she describes this memory as the mesmerizing and terrorizing image of the "hand." The subject here feels deep acquaintance, and more than acquaintance with "my dark haired // dark eyed bogey man, / my monster, // my stranger." She knows and wants to keep this man, not expose him and lose him forever. After a moment's hesitation, however, her new strength drives her on to sing further revelations.

> no use shutting the door,
>
> he's made of air.
> though he was real
>
> flesh & blood once,
> my monster man,

that first time,
in grandma's house

in Rosengart,
in grandma's bed, (76)

An adult male attacks and almost kills the little child in her own
grandmother's house.

wolf in sheep's clothing
(though still her child)

making the room spin,
dissolving walls & floor,

my life flickering
at the ceiling,

off, on, off, on.

Peter's hands on my throat,
death hands, full of hate,

his penis a hammer
in my mouth. (76-77)

Now, for the first time in this book, possibly in all of Brandt's
books, she makes use of a dotted line to separate this last entry
from the succeeding one, as if to say, "Now it is done. I am finished. The story is told, finally."

The particular act of oppression in the poet's life finally reveals
itself, the man's name given and recorded forever, even the complicity of a whole ancestry publicized. Little remains for the poet
now to wring out in this account of her loveless upbringing and
bare survival but to draw a deep breath of relief, and sum things up.

his penis a hammer
in my mouth

. . . .

i've lived my life
with courage, & great terror.

i've walked through fire.
i've learned to spell death

backwards,
heat, hate, hat, head.

i've been sung to by angels.
mit Rosen bedacht.

finding the lost child
in me, after such dying,

knowing everything,
miracle baby,

mit heisser Liebe,
unharmed. (77)

The ellipsis indicates the boundary between the lost child and
the past, and the reborn child and the present. The reborn child
brought about rebirth because it began to speak the truth and
fought off the desire to serve the very force that violated her.
Standing outside the history of violence herself, her own involvement has been the victim's desire to associate with power, since
power protects as well as harms.

This "once real" event of the rape of the infant—identifiable
in the following poem as the "bad" girl, the baby girl, the "wild,
spirit child," the "naughty one," the "wildflower, weed" (*mother,
not mother* 80)—represents for the narrator the quintessence of
male violence, that particular manifestation of it that forced her
to learn to love her enemy. That is to say, the rape has forced her
to live so long with the fear of "Peter's" dreadfulness, the shame
of his imposition on her, and the hollowness of personal weakness and impotence as a result of his great physical chastisement
of her in her weak, vulnerable infancy. The "Old Story" successfully retold, however, she now may find herself at liberty to discover the "real" identity of the cowering inner child.

In the poem beginning "sometimes" in *mother, not mother*, as
I have said, she claims to have experienced much in her life, now
having come to a sort of full and complete state of knowing.

i've been sung to by angels.
mit Rosen bedacht.

finding the lost child
in me, after such dying

knowing everything
miracle baby (77)

Much earlier, in *questions i asked my mother*, the poet sets out
on a heroic quest; appropriately, the writer has studied archetypal theory (the theory of the hero in literature) from Northrop
Frye himself. Brandt says about this period of her studies that
"Frye's grand archetypal vision had given me a framework in
which to make sense of the bewildering array of stories that make
up the body we call literature, but it was useless for coming to
terms with maternal experience" (*Wild Mother Dancing* 3).

one time i asked her about bread   i loved smelling the
brown yeast in the huge blue speckled bowl its sweetish
ferment watching it bubble & churn how does it turn into
bread i asked her   well the yeast is what makes it rise she
said when you add warm water it grows as you can see yes
but how does it turn into bread i mean it comes out a completely different thing what exactly happens to it in there in
the oven why does heat turn it into something full of holes
we can eat   she sighed my mother sighed a lot when i was
around   you're asking me something i can't tell you she said
now help me punch down the dough   i sat in front of the
oven all afternoon bathed in warm kitchen smells trying to
figure it out someday i said to myself someday i will find out
i will find out everything (*questions* 7)

The "everything" she eventually succeeds in discovering takes her
out of this warm and cozy kitchen and through a world of terror
to a point of exhaustion. The word "punch," in this otherwise
innocuous account of a youngster querying a busy mother in a
pretty kitchen, hints at the dangers of the journey to come.

This will be a heroic quest, with all the danger and contest
heroes face and manage. The poet's quest is heroic despite
Brandt's disclaimer in *mother, not mother*: "she does not hate //
her charred / womanskin. // she does not long / for a hero" (72).

Above, the dough rising, of course, suggests the baby rising and growing in the womb, in the warm, close, pleasant womb much like the kitchen. The questions the child wishes to ask represent the world of dangers and senses the individual must experience outside the "loving" home of father and mother. Brandt tells us that her problems with archetypal (i.e., academic, current scholarly) explanations for maternal narrative began in 1976 with the birth of her first child, and continued through to the last book she wrote.

> Meanwhile [after 1976], I began to write poetry, circling around the question of the absent mother, exploring the mother's problematic absence/presence in language intuitively, rhythmically, through sound and image. Through the writing of three consecutive volumes, *questions i asked my mother* (1987), *Agnes in the sky* (1990), and *mother, not mother* (1992), I began to formulate the argument of this book, supported by current feminist theory, notably that of Adrienne Rich, Mary Daly, Julia Kristeva, Luce Irigaray and Marianne Hirsch, that the mother has been so largely absent in Western narrative, not because she is unnarratable, but because her subjectivity has been violently, and repeatedly, suppressed. (*Wild Mother Dancing* 7)

The father and mother here in the early reaches of her family narrative represent only minor deterritorializing forces. These forces inexorably push the subject away from the "real" and safe linguistic environment of some maternal territory in that, as we have seen, the mother in her ignorance of science (farm wife that she is) cannot tell her much about the factors of leavening, while the father criticizes her, calling her contrary and willful when she questions the Bible's account of the last judgement:

> i don't think that's a very
> nice thing to say about grampa she begins   she wouldn't say
> this if we were alone it's an introduction   she lets him
> finish with the big stuff   it's your attitude he says i've
> noticed lately everything you say has this questioning tone i
> don't think you're really interested in grampa or your faith
> what you really want is to make trouble for mom & me
> you've always been like that you're always trying to figure
> everything out your own way instead of submitting quietly
> to the teachings of the church when are you going to learn

> not everything has to make sense your brain is not the most
> important thing in the world what counts is your attitude &
> your faith your willingness to accept the mystery of God's
> ways (*questions i asked my mother* 5-6)

Accusation of disobedience both to parents and to God has a
long history for her. Her father is depicted earlier as ignorant and
irrational, resenting his daughter's desire to test the truths he
accepts.

> but what do you think my father says this verse means if it's
> not about the end of the world look that's obviously a mis-
> reading i say the verb grammatically speaking doesn't have
> an object in this instance so it can't possibly be made to
> that's exactly what i mean he says waving the book in mid
> air if my father ever shouted he would be shouting now you
> don't really care about the meaning all you ever think about
> is grammar & fancy words i never even heard of where i
> come from the reason you learn to read is to understand
> God's Holy Word i only went to school 7 years & it's done
> me okay what are you going to do with all this hifalutin
> education anyway don't you think it's time you got a job &
> did some honest work for a change (4)

The father's anger at his daughter focusses on those aspects of her
character that think against the simple Mennonite understanding of truth. Her father takes no time out to enjoy the pleasure
of the world of the senses. Pleasure taken in the earth is, for
religious simpletons, a waste of time, or at best a dangerous
diversion.

The poet, as poets are wont and known to do, longs for pleasure. She hungers for a heaven, centred right here in an inviting
world that includes the warm kitchen smells and sensations, and
also the earth outside the kitchen.

> when i was five i thought heaven was located
> in the hayloft of our barn the ladder to get
> up there was straight & narrow like the Bible
> said if you fell off you might land on the
> horns of a cow or be smashed on cement the men
> in the family could leap up in seconds wielding
> pitchforks my mother never even tried for us
> children it was hard labour (2)

A lovely materiality characterizes the little narrator girl's vision of heaven. If heaven cannot be felt and seen like this, it cannot be heaven. Heaven must have all the charming mythic qualities of the stories we have inherited, as well as all the prettiness of the earth we have spent our years close to, if it has any hope of appealing to a thinking person as a reasonable heaven.

> i was the scaredy
> i couldn't reach the first rung so i stood at
> the bottom & imagined what heaven was like there
> was my grandfather with his Santa Claus beard
> sitting on a wooden throne among straw bales
> never saying a word but smiling & patting us
> on the head & handing out bubble gum to those
> who were good even though his eyes were half
> closed he could see right inside your head (2)

Santa is God, the ladder takes the place of the classic narrow path up to heaven, which sinners find so difficult to climb (see even here the connection to Patrick Friesen's "bannister" to heaven), the throne is a pile of straw bales, believably regal because baled straw has the most yellow sheen, which, to a child's eye, could naturally appear to be a golden throne, the mythic God is kind and loving, especially to children, and he proves it in her imagination by his gifts of bubble gum and patting them on the head, he does not speak to his subjects in the Bible, nor here in the hayloft, and, significantly for the poet's later life, he is omniscient, seeing all the thoughts going on in her head even with his eyes half-closed.

Her feelings concerning God and heaven, even material as they are, cannot escape the simple truth of her unworthiness her pious father has already, at this tender age, drummed into her:

> i squirmed my way to the back of the line &
> unwished the little white lie i had told which
> i could feel growing grimy up there & tried
> not to look at the dark gaping hole where they
> shoved out black sinners like me (2)

Immediately, however, in the moment of self-loathing, another beatific vision replaces this dark one of hell and damnation. The power and beauty of Brandt's poetry cannot be felt anywhere more than in the passage that follows. That special quality is the vulnerability of the poet here who allows herself to be Memory." The philosopher Martin Heidegger connects thanks and memory in *What Is Called Thinking:*

> Both memory and thanks move and have their being in the *thanc.* 'Memory' initially did not at all mean the power to recall. The word designates the whole disposition in the sense of a steadfast intimate concentration upon the things that essentially speak to us in every thoughtful meditation. (140)

To be vulnerable memory is to think hard about the past without excluding the painful parts—being thankful for them, in fact—and those painful parts always include the complicity of the subject in the "problem." To be memory is to be any one of a subject's past constructions with openness and with feelings unbridled. The little girl here, tentative in the presence of her very strong brothers who can leap up the hayloft ladder in a second, fearful of the things that can fall down out of that black hole, unexplainably finds "wonders" falling from there, and not only people of the "black sinner" sort. She is fearful, she is, dare I say it, sweet, she is intrigued with and blessed by the tiny. Not large heavens (of the sort she needs later, for instance, in "each cell" in *Jerusalem, beloved* 47) alone are necessary, nor grand signs of heavenness, but "tiny blue flowerets pressed / on dry stems." The girl's fragility and tenderness, her need for small, particular tenderness rather than glorious systems of general goodness in God, and her innocence and sad (though pretty) love are presented here in as effective a poetry as anyone could hope for:

> but the best
> part was the smell of new pitched hay wafting
> about some of it fell to where i stood under
> the ladder there were tiny blue flowerets pressed
> on dry stems i held them to my nose & breathed
> deep sky & sun it was enough heaven for me for
> one day (2)

She is aware at her tender age, to the instant outrage in the sensitive reader against propaganda, of her sinfulness. Yet, she hungers for the lovely and kind. She senses in some dim part of her green subjectivity the cruelty which the Pretty endures, "pressed" as it is and "dried" in its short duration. The replacement in these lines of the dark for the light, the rich and desiring earth for the wicked repressiveness of heaven, indicates early in her first book the precise longing the poet feels throughout her childhood and growing years. This materiality she has loved as a young girl, and which she has obviously incorporated in a spiritual sense with Santa, flowers, hay, and other produce of our earth and earth's culture, has eluded her as a growing woman. She has felt focussed on the name of the father instead of on the earth; she has felt confined and imprisoned by the memory of the wicked "hand" (*mother, not mother* 28) from which she only finds release decades later because of the love and wisdom of the woman who touches her into new life; she has felt cheated of life's innocence by the violence of men, a violence represented in the early phase of *questions i asked my mother* by the niggling and ignorance-loving father in the passage I have already glossed and others of similar autobiographical intent and effect. In sum, Brandt effectively paints a picture of the loveliness of the earth, and of the young girl who loves her earth so much, robbed of that love by the "monster" (*mother, not mother* 76) who insists that God cannot be and must not be Santa Claus, and that his heaven must be "understood" (*questions i asked my mother* 4) more than felt.

Much later, after having understood everything, "understanding" standing for a weak and miserable form of knowing the earth, the poet reflects on that part played in her long quest by the infant girl who refused to be pinched and wrung into a mechanical version of her father's subjectivity.

> little one, black angel,
> disobedient, wilful,
>
> wild, spirit child.
> you wouldn't die.
>
> you wouldn't take
> the family lie

into your mouth,
your belly,

the nasty secret,
wouldn't keep it. (*mother, not mother* 80)

All the literary markers point to Wordsworth's "Lucy Gray" (already also pointed to in Friesen's work), whose parents too have treated her with great efficiency and heaven-bound coldness, and who appears to have died at the end of that poem trying to please them. In Brandt's case, the child, "wild" and "spirited," just like Lucy Gray who takes the lantern into town on an errand commissioned by her father on a bitter winter's night and who gets lost in a blizzard—possibly as a way of answering a question often asked about Wordsworth's imaginary child—refuses to die and lives by learning to speak the truth about the lie the family has perpetrated. This lie concerns, as I mentioned earlier, the violent rape of the child on her grandmother's bed, which the family refuses to believe, but also the lie the father insists upon that God and all spirituality are immaterial and beyond the world of touch. The materiality of the means by which the poet eventually finds freedom from the father's (the family's) lie now appears to our sight more clearly: the woman who strokes the "broken-winged" girl in *mother, not mother* (27ff) brings about her rebirth through touch (the material is nothing if it is not touch); rebirth itself speaks plainly about coming into life through passages of flesh and bone, coming from silence to crying, coming from warmth to coldness and other equally sensual, tactile qualities.

I have said this little girl's vulnerability makes "questions i asked my mother," as well as the other poems in this book, great. Vulnerability, however, is not just or simply innocence. In "Marian makes lists" the poet's vulnerability takes a set of characteristics entirely opposite from innocence and purity. Marian is a woman (sister of the poet, older cousin or playmate, married aunt, we do not know) who keeps careful tally of things to be remembered: groceries to buy, chores to be done by such and such a day, acquaintances' birthdays, the cost of household necessities. All these innocuous items Marian arranges in her mind in obeisance to proper domesticity. All these items to be remembered would be things a good housewife in 1940s and 1950s southern Manitoba Mennoniteville would have been expected to learn to organize with care and efficiency. The poet, however, admits her proclivity for lists of another sort:

> me i
> carry around this list of things i can't forgive
> the time my mother made me stand in the corner by
> the basement steps & my cousin Joyce came over &
> i had to pretend i was so engrossed in *Reader's*
> *Digest* i wasn't the slightest bit interested in
> going bike riding with her & the sun shining first
> time in a week or the time my sister got sucked
> into raising her hand at evangelical meeting & she
> had to get counselling from the deacon behind the
> coat rack after church or my brother pulling the
> wings off sparrows & swinging the cat by its tail
> just to make us scream & my mother always thinking
> he was a saint & my dad grotesquely cheerful after
> milking barging into the room with his grin & good
> morning & we with our awkward limbs only half dressed
> oh yes like Marian i remember my family i tally up
> prices i keep track (*questions i asked my mother* 3)

The best qualities of Brandt's poetry go into the construction of this poem. There is here a materiality of the sort "when i was five" brought to our attention. The spiritual is brought down from its loft and contacted only at the level of the movements and speeds the *constructed* version of the spiritual spins into being here on earth, such as her sister's unfortunate consequence in the coat room for "raising up her hand" at the altar call. Notice the image here is not of a raising of the spirit, or a raising of the mind or consciousness, nor any other sorts of quasi-spiritual yearnings heavenward, but a raising of hands. Patrick Friesen, in contrast, features feet in his hinge poem in *The Shunning*. Hands play such an important role in Brandt's account of her becoming-poet so the introduction here of hands in this strongly material way at an evangelical revival meeting, which is to say in the very site of twentieth century Mennonite spirituality, threads materiality all the way through her text, even those parts that seem to lapse into a feminist spirituality or essentiality as insistent (and non-economical, non-productive) as an "evangelical meeting." The material use of hands in place of hearts and minds and spirits here shows us how subversive hands may be and generally forces us to expect the tearing down of, rather than the raising up of, the spiritual edifice by hands whenever we will meet them in Brandt's poetry.

But the despiritualizing, materializing, deterritorializing use of "hand" constitutes only one minor way in which this poem reveals its high material standards, in which this poem makes itself vulnerable. The materiality of Brandt's writing without compromise lives here in these lines, then, purely impure and constructed and social; so much of the material culture of Mennonite life swims on the surface of this poem. But—and partly and—her willingness to tell all as she thinks it, with such telling's incompleteness or even minor existence outside the text, also breathes here. She is angry. She dislikes her father's grinning (duplicitous) insinuation of himself into the girls' bedroom where they are changing. She "tall[ies] up" and "keep[s] track" with exaggerated annoyance and obsessive willfulness. She imagines in poetic ways not the good and beautiful (and so really very lyrical and useless to poetry in effect), sentimental, imposed, metaphysical, prettified worlds for the consumption of those who cannot face life's dying with authenticity. But rather she imagines her home-world with authentic and material accuracy, impervious to the glossing tendency of most imaginers to paint themselves well, or paint the world well, or paint themselves and their world well (teleologically). She is impervious as well to love/joy/beatificity/pleasure/praise/assurance/final well-being and all those other forms of pretending that basically all is well with the world, as the lyric poet makes it for his readers to help take their minds off their own "good" and constant dying (which is determined by them to be fearful and duplicitous, with agency, when it is nothing more than dying, when there is no doubleness, or darkness, for that matter, in it whatsoever. Death is simply that, not more than itself, or bigger than any other thing. Donne tried to say this with, "Death, once dead, there's no more dying then." Death has no subjectivity).

Brandt professes complicity in evil, to make a short point of it. That is, she does not label evil as "evil" here, but instead refrains from binary judgement with this complicit and real text. Therein lies the most effective form of her vulnerability. Such ethical "self"-implication constitutes an ethics of the most engaging sort. Brandt's material poem here takes the double naming (giving phenomena/events transcendent value and agency; all events are material, without significance) out of dying and leaves it in its singleness, as Nietzsche has taught us to do:

> For, just as popular superstition divorces the lightning from its brilliance, viewing the latter as an activity whose subject is the lightning, so does popular morality divorce strength from its manifestations, as though there were behind the strong a neutral agent, free to manifest its strength or contain it. But no such agent exists; there is no "being" behind the doing, acting, becoming; the "does" has simply been added to the deed by the imagination—the doing is everything. The common man actually doubles the doing by making the lightning flash; he states the same event once as cause and then again as effect. The natural scientists are no better when they say "energy *moves*," "energy **causes**." For all its detachment and freedom from emotion, our science is still the dupe of linguistic habits; it has never yet got rid of those changelings called "subjects." The atom is one such changeling, another is the Kantian "thing-in-itself." Small wonder, then, that the repressed and smoldering emotions of vengeance and hatred have taken advantage of this superstition and in fact espouse no belief more ardently than that it is within the discretion of the strong to be weak, of the bird of prey to be a lamb. (*Genealogy of Morals* 178-79)

Notice especially the word "common." It is a common and vulgar (cowardly/showing no personal history of restraint) practice to make the effect the cause as if these were two separate entities and with subjective agency. This piece of Nietzsche's precisely states, in an originary way, Deleuze's later claim that history happens "behind the thinker's back," despite the questions we ask. We say our plans, our revolutionary aims, our great revolts, are caused by our idealism, our grand questions, our causes. They are not. These questions insist that the strong can be made weak, that the belief in something affects the outcome of things and states, and improves them. The minor (persons with causes writing for this or that group), however, influences the major in its own incalculable ways; history happens behind our backs in its own way; the flows that are history spread out in patterns that can be recognized as patterns, not as plans. Brandt's revolutionary intent will never bring about predictable results, or any kind of useful results. Unpredictable changes will simply come about because of this exposure of flows, which have usually been kept secret (by a group, a territory, and its lyrical spokespersons) and always thought of as "permanent structure."

Brandt's poetic child is angry and she hates the ones who have annoyed her in her youthful years. She is herself more violent and abusive in her compulsive keeping of lists than her siblings, relatives, or parents have been in their various actions. This violence replacing love here (and the father's grinning intrusion suggests love more than it suggests deviousness), this poet's nit-picking replacing larger, loving, forgiving, relating sensibilities possessed by the others in her family tell us that *the poet* is the one about whom lists should rightfully be kept. In effect, she doubles their actions and makes those actions passive. She thus falsifies the documents, falsifies history, orders history along lines that allow her to make forms of flows, to make double what was single, to make a subject with agency what only *occurred* (motion, not stasis), and to make the effect also the cause. She accumulates a secret history of evils here and in doing so *makes* these innocent actions passive, memorialized evils.

Not only does she *act* as a list-keeper, she *knows* at some level that she does this, that *she* is duplicitous, that she is the perpetrator of the making of minor annoyances into major ills. She is, the poet makes public, the poet broadcasts in a way only minor literature usually has the courage to do, the originator of evils in the family, in history. This self-problematization, this neurotic sense of her own culpability, this combining of love and violence, this consideration of vulnerability as hatred, this airing of the minor group's politics, makes this poem, and many others in *questions i asked my mother,* among the best poems Brandt has written. This vulnerability, which is self-problematization, makes "Marian makes lists" among the best poems written, not only among Mennonites, of course—not that many of this sort from this group have been written—but the best on the Canadian prairies and in Canada. They are of the best, if vulnerability, which is a non-linguistic, subjective quality, is conceded to be evidence of fine writing.

Di Brandt's writing is minor writing. It has a high coefficient of deterritorialization (albeit a "rich," and so ineffectively minor, deterritorialization which actually is a reterritorialization), it automatically speaks for community values (even when she speaks against them), and it is visibly political. She is minor over against the major. She is a revolutionary user of English even when she attempts to use it in non-revolutionary ways. In other words, Brandt's poetry does not, in the style of Kafka, the deterritorializer of German, who relentlessly subverts the conventions of the major language in which he writes, deliberately impoverish English at every turn, but she does so accidentally. She does so accidentally because she strives to write a poetry acceptably great in its allusiveness and lyrical strength, restrained in its expression, economic in its suggestivness, symbolically rich, in other words, in the conventions of major writing. She practises a poetry of symbolic reterritorialization and so is *de facto* not deliberately subversive of the major. Accidental impoverishment of English (deterritorialization of English) just as effectively reforms that language as does deliberate impoverishment. Paradoxically, besides this accidental minor quality, and symptomatic of it, her poetry is actually major in that her models, as I have said earlier, are the great poets.

Brandt's is the poetry of anger, poetry of the cause, of the political purpose, of the revolutionary agenda. Typically, where there is revolution, there is belief. We have this or that to prove. The revolution wishes for this or that to occur because it believes strongly in this or that human virtue or value. Neither the specific wish nor the specific value or virtue will be fulfilled or finally honoured. It is not the revolution's belief that will be legitimized in the end, but another unpredictable new state that will be the visible recipient of these efforts at change. Yet, fulfillment and honour of a sort, in the form of the new, will result. The minor text, bravely rebelling and loudly calling for this or that change, exposes itself in public, and this self-exposure, this humble act of letting all see everything without great secrecy, forces the major text to come temporarily to terms with its arrogance and its desire for secrecy (secrecy by an entity being always a desire to interpret its own text as a divine one, a transcendental signifier), and in the process a new relationship is formed between groups. Big groups yield to small groups and the balance of power, the balance of prohibitions, the balance of have

and have not, the balance of the apparent permanence of institutions, the balance of all large and complacent groups' relations
to small and politically active groups, shifts, changes, evolves,
moves materially through a series of physical states (which would
always seek to remain non-moving if it were up to the big, non-
revolutionary group).

Brandt's anger will not bring about any political change or any
value system she may think worthy, but it will bring about
change. All minor writing does. Without her anger and that of
other minor voices, English literature, with its cultural hegemony and its unified field of big groups and large social organiza-
tions, would not see (embarrassed) its own selfish/secret/power-
ful politics hidden and kept underground in a sort of basement,
or unconscious, as if a destined force and a destined state. There
is no unconscious; there are only secret agendas. The unconscious, site of the unexpressed self, is an essentialist image of the
subject, which cannot be valid unless we believe (in the fashion
of all causes) that a transcendent being has made each one of us
different and unique, and that we each potentially have a great
service to perform in that "being's" will. Without such a transcendent view of the "being" of the subject, and with another
view of the subject which sees it wholly constructed and different only insofar as it has encountered a unique combination of
discourses and desiring objects over time and within conditions
of speed, this subject has no more a personal, undiscovered,
unique personhood than does each unique snowflake. Brandt's
minor anger changes major power, though never in any way she
wishes it to or towards a goal she may have in mind. Brandt's
minor English literature—her rallying of snowflakes—changes
major English literature whether it wishes such particular
changes or not. Without Brandt's minor English inscriptions, as
I have said before, major English literature would stand still and
spin its wheels, unable as it is on its own to vitally criticize the
false assumptions, lies and transcendental signification it constructs into its systems and institutions as if they were uncon-
structed and from on high. I use "high" here to suggest constructed "hierarchy," which hegemony always invokes as a model
of proper relations. In an ideal age in which hegemony has been
defeated, hierarchical imagery will no longer have potency and

currency and a new age of horizontal relations will predominate. This is, I think, going to be, when thought of in sociological terms, an age of community (global, possibly), in theological terms, an age of brotherhood and love, and in political terms, an age in little need of a government or of complex leadership. See Gonzalo's speech in Shakespeare's *The Tempest*. Such a non-hegemonic age sounds positively utopian.

The lesson in the above thinking is clear. The personal and political ends that drive our writing are dispensable. The state that comes out of our writing is not recognizable from a profile or prediction or chart drawn based on the specifics of our convictions. Texts have minds (desiring directions) of their own. Groups have minds (desiring directions) of their own. Writers are not in charge of the ethics or changes in ethics that groups undergo. Writers are not in charge of a dynamic that is essentially material and not spiritual. Writers are exposers of the materiality, the non-spirituality, of the dynamics of groups in that they are exposers of the essential and utter materiality of writing itself. Writing, whether it wishes to be so or not, is deconstructive. It is the trace that leaves for others to see, the presence that leaves for others to see, the other logic, the "false" logic in all values, the "false" logic in all representations, the "false" logic in all agreements and truths. False the logic is not; it is simply other than and constructed via its peculiar combinations of historico-linguistic elements and impulses. In the history of language the Western world is caught in, logic and anything else can be said to be "false," as opposite to "true," but all today already know this, though they are not yet and will not be till the end of the age of subjectivity in a desiring position to construct new and non-ontological categories that tell of the constructed, material nature of the concepts (cause/effects) by which an epoch simplifies its thinking. In this age, the true/false binary has allowed us to grow up and raise up others without a memory, that is to say without an inclination toward thankfulness, recalling Heidegger's link between thanks and memory. Di Brandt's anger may as well be as not be an anger. It is just one of the ways the "false" in logic makes itself known. Her anger is a "falsehood." Her anger is a writing. Her anger is a minor anger and in that it is very powerful. It is, despite the scepticism I can hear from critics who say, "We know that," worth repeating, since the "false" is always easily forgotten, especially by the reader who wishes to see the "false" as "true." She wishes the secure and the permanent to be the way the universe works. The reader may as well as not be reminded that the security he smacks his lips over is neither security nor particularly more pleasureful than insecurity. Insecurity holds all the cards, in fact. To remember the "falseness" of all claims to "truth" is to have pleasure. I think.

6.

Mennonites and Métis in the Never Never of Agassiz: Sandra Birdsell's Waste Land Territory

Sandra Birdsell most strongly retains her minor status in her address of political problems. She speaks for a particular minor group, a very small group, the Aboriginal Canadian/Mennonite Canadian group of southern Manitoba. No other fiction writer has emerged from this precise language grouping. That happens to be, most likely, because so few subjects belong to it. Possibly only a few dozen families in Canada have a Mennonite Canadian/Aboriginal Canadian territorial subjectivity. The mixture of the European and the North American territories makes for fascinating writing. Her impact as a writer comes from her awareness of the troublesome mixture of the two systems of codes, the two territories, within one family; the Lafreniere family in *Night Travellers* represents this union. Birdsell's power, however, also derives from the interaction within her work of the minor and the major in literature. The Mennonite literary subject is both major and minor, of European, classical, intellectual, Western history by association, but out of it by its history of dissociation from most of the West's major codes.

The Aboriginal Canadian literary subject generally must be labelled minor because of its non-European territorial memories and its history of resistance to, as well as its hopes for acceptance by, major Canadian literature. The Aboriginal Canadian subject sees himself as always outside the mainstream Canadian text. See Thomas King's *Medicine River* and *Green Grass, Running Water,* Jordan Wheeler's *Brothers in Arms,* and Ruby Slipperjack's *Honour the Sun,* for instance. Greek/Roman/Judeo-Christian intellectual history is never effectively alluded to in their texts. The Mennonite Canadian subject, on the other hand, sees himself as inside the mainstream Canadian text and outside it at the same time for a complex set of reasons. Rudy Wiebe's Thom in *Peace Shall Destroy Many* belongs in Canada spatially and to a degree politically, but religiously opposes the Canadian war efforts and so feels seriously "other" than the "ordinary" Canadian. Armin Wiebe's characters, such as Yasch in *The Salvation of Yasch Siemens,* are, by their Low German language and Mennonite rural roots, separate from the "Robertson Davies" literary textual society, which presumes a non-political world of busy, universal, social-intellectual interchange, and yet, European and Middle Eastern Christianity have given all Mennonite Canadian literary subjects a common intellectual history which they themselves feel substantially part of (Menno Simons being one of the great thinkers of the Anabaptists). And on and on, Mennonite Canadians always feel separate from and united with other Canadians. Sandra Birdsell's writing presents the combination of these two political, material territories within one voice. Her overall contribution may be characterized as a deterritorializing of both Aboriginal Canadian and Mennonite Canadian minor territories in her earlier work, represented by the collection of stories entitled *Night Travellers,* and then an attempt at a deterritorialization of major territoriality in her two novels, *The Missing Child* and *The Chrome Suite.*

In *Night Travellers,* Maurice Lafreniere is an ordinary working man in Agassiz whom the bankers, town administrators, and other middle-class townspeople treat shabbily, partly because of his lowly occupation of barbering, his coarseness of language and dress, and his profligacy, but mainly because of his Métis blood. His mother has been found literally dead drunk, and the town holds that against him as much as it considers such an event typical of his kind: "It would have turned out well if it hadn't been that it took too long for a town to forget a person who would die suffocating on their own vomit" (*Night Travellers* 14). The implications are clear enough in this comment, but the racism that crushes basically good people like Maurice comes to him much more directly, sometimes hypocritically as a "kindness" done by the redneck. A local friend of his confidentially *reminds* him of the inferiority of Métis culture: "Don't let anyone tell you different, Henry Roy had said, mongrels don't make better dogs" (15).

Maurice's wife, being Mennonite, experiences no such difficulties finding acceptance: "The town would rush in for a woman like Mika. The town thought Mika had taken him in hand and with her clean habits and Mennonite ways had made him what he was today" (2). All the stories in Birdsell's long and short fiction come down hard on the convention of the protected and pampered mother. Mothers find credibility far too easily when often—almost universally, if Birdsell's drama is to be believed—they whine, hit, yell, reject, and generally do little to earn the approbation and automatic respect they get. This alienating mother contrasts with Di Brandt's mothers, who are usually wonderful, or at least wonders. Mika treats Maurice much the way Roy believes Métis should be treated, as some lower form of being, when clearly in some respects he garners the reader's greater respect: of the two he parents more effectively; he loves his children; he respects his wife; he bears his wife's idiosyncrasies with long-suffering, despite her vicious anger at him and her weariness of being mother to her children (*Night Travellers* 74). Unwanted, Maurice nevertheless tries hard with a commendable persistence, the stories explain, to fit in.

Partly due to his marginal social status in the town, Maurice has long wanted to give some proof of his importance and value as a member of the community. He eventually gets his wish. When the worst flood in recorded history inundates Agassiz, it turns out that Maurice predicted it:

> Old Man River. That was the name they'd given to him since his prediction of the flood had come true. Maurice Lafreniere reads the river like it was a newspaper. When the going gets tough, the tough gets going, he told himself. And he'd proven himself. (7)

Maurice's humdrum life on the margin of things in Agassiz

seems about to turn interesting and important. The possibility of progress and new purpose seems to be held out to him with his fortuitous prediction and he intends to take advantage of it: "Why do you have to stay, now of all times, Mika had asked. And he couldn't explain to her that for once he didn't want to be on the outside, left out, but dead centre" (7). Maurice now suddenly sports a widespread local credibility, to the chagrin of businessmen like Mayor Livingston, who grabs every opportunity to discredit Maurice. Medley, a reporter from Winnipeg, come to investigate the damage done by the flood, clearly indicates that he prefers to record Maurice's instead of local officials' opinions concerning the catastrophe. Livingston interrupts Maurice's claim that controlling floods might be a possibility in the future: "[W]e could take steps to make certain that this here flood will never happen again" (12). Livingston laughs insultingly and with magisterial pomp points out some particular flood damage to Medlake. Sensing, however, what officials in Agassiz have never wished to sense—Maurice's perspicacity and good sense— Medlake quietly admonishes Livingston, asking him to [w]ait, let him finish" (13). His credibility established in Agassiz in this way, his credibility for the reader also rises.

Maurice wants recognition and acceptance from the leaders of the community, however, not just from reporters. The desire for official acceptance constitutes the particular flaw in his character, I would probably think if I were reading a work such as *The Rime of the Ancient Mariner*, *Frankenstein*, *The Lady of Shalott*, or *Hamlet*. That judgement might not be so far from the mark, despite the late-twentieth-century status of this story. Maurice tragically dies at the end of *Night Travellers* without completing the great symbolic boat-building project he fiddled with for half his life, one that fortified him against the continual disappointments of social and domestic rejection. Temporarily, however, Maurice's desire finds satisfaction. He warns Livingston in Medley's presence of the immediate susceptibility of the courthouse basement walls to the rising pressure of the groundwater. Livingston, at least, disbelieves him, claiming with disdain that the walls are two feet thick and impervious. Then the walls cave immediately upon our Canadian Livingston's denial, just after they've entered the building, significantly immediately after

Maurice refuses Livingston's boorish demand that he "say something to them in Indian" (15).

> "In a pig's ass," Maurice said, his anger breaking loose in upraised fists. The floor beneath him tilted. And then there was a sound, like thunder, beneath them. Relief flooded every part of his body and his knees suddenly felt weak. He felt like laughing hysterically. (15)

The walls come tumbling down, not unlike those of Jericho in that classical Old Testament vindication of Israel. The miraculous exists in Birdsell's world. This timely intervention signals nature's sympathy for special people. The miraculous exists. It honours its beloved, the downtrodden, particularly the Aboriginal downtrodden. This combination of affects and effects, though textual, does not have the "feel" about it of careful planning. It sounds suspiciously as if it sympathizes exactly with Birdsell's own desire for a "unicorn" power in a world that, as she increasingly shows, seldom *reveals* that wondrous facet of cosmic flows and movements. In the readers' experiences, babies about to be abandoned are not picked up and delivered to the Salvation Army's doorsteps, good-hearted drunks on Henry Street are not covered in blankets from the frost when it dips to thirty below at night, and no matter how worthy of protection, young women about to be done some violence to are not mysteriously protected by an angel hand or a "thunder"-voiced heavenly being in the way that Maurice here is backed in his political ambitions by Nature.

Despite the existence in his world of a mysterious force, which provides for its subjects (not unlike Di Brandt's in *Jerusalem, beloved* 47), Maurice pays no attention to his own consequent potential as a favourite of the spiritual. The cosmos loves him and comes to his aid; he rejects that special spirit and finally, as narrative time evolves, makes a flop of his life. We do not know that his life would not have been ordinary with kind Nature's assistance, had he believed and remembered her goodness, but we know that, not believing or remembering her advocacy of him here during the flood, he more or less peters out. He loses energy and friends; he continues to try to fit into White society but fails. He behaves in all the ways that bode ill for him if he wishes to be happier.

It is this ultra-ordinary impulse in subjects that Birdsell's stories impress upon her readers. Betty, Truda, Lureen, Maurice, Mika, and others all are shown at moments of crisis and choice but in every case each of them chooses badly, or, we could say, chooses for that course of action that will lead her down an increasingly sad, lonely, and misunderstood path. This refusal of the miraculous by each subject at every narrated moment in every one of her stories and novels, in other words, is the norm for the ordinary in her work, even if that miraculous element in the world represents simply the potential for the individual to feel important and worthwhile. The ordinary fails to recognize the extraordinary right there before it. The ordinary subject, therefore, must experience because of this neglect the opposite of the miraculous, namely a slide, a steady, precipitous slide down into great discouragement. Only two possibilities exist in Birdsell's work, both hierarchical: the climbing happy, or the declining unhappy. The ordinary that sees itself as ordinary and celebrates the ordinary, looking forward to the next office party, political convention, Winnipeg Folk Festival, family gathering, winter vacation in Arizona, shift in the weather, and so on, never occurs. Events must be highly dramatic in Birdsell's work. Birdsell's narrative possibilities must represent extreme affirmation or denial. The author knows another possibility, of course. She shows us potential for celebration in the ordinary world. Unlike her, however, her subjects fail to see. Blind, they rush headlong toward disaster and annihilation.

These traits, these slippages into alienation, derive from the conventions of high modernism: the *eironic* author (a Socratic term) who knows more than her characters; the extraordinary real universe; the shortsighted and unknowing, willful, wrong-choosing subject; and the wasteland clearly visible at the end of the story. This combination of high alienation due to subjective ignorance and an inability to visualize possibilities or miracles determines the plots, settings, characters, points of view, and themes of all the stories Birdsell writes. Miracle and ignorance of miracle are both present, even when one of the two does not appear to be explicitly there. This particular simultaneous presence characterizes most of the short stories of *Night Travellers*. When the story presents a downward movement, when a character chooses badly or chooses what will further alienate her from loved ones, or when relationships reach an impasse, with no particular extraordinary cause to account for it in the story, the element of the miraculous nevertheless lives there in the silence, in what the author leaves unsaid, possibly determined by something supra-natural which earlier entered the narrative.

The family with whom the short stories of *Night Travellers* concern themselves includes Maurice, a Métis man married, as I have said, to Mika, a Russian-Mennonite immigrant who intensely dislikes her husband's lower-class values, especially his general sloppiness and his tendency to drink and stay out late. When it comes to orderly living, he is not German; that is certain. They have children, Betty, Lureen, and Truda, each featured in one or more of the book's stories. Tensions between their parents twist and hurt the children (predictably for realist fiction conventions, which always see only one possibility for the nuclear family). The children reflect the dysfunctionality of their parents' marriage in the sorts of decisions they make in their own relationships, in their thinking, and in their hopes for meaning. Two other important members of the extended family are the Mennonite Grandmother and Grandfather Thiessen, whose own relationship, though it appears normal and calm to the children, contains terrible conflicts that can never be resolved and so secretly contribute to the dissolution of the Lafreniere family.

In "The Wednesday Circle," fourteen-year-old Betty Lafreniere reluctantly goes to a farm neighbour's place for eggs, knowing she will be fondled by the old and (again typical of realist fiction, which idealizes youth and protects it with a complex moral system) repulsive Mr. Joy, an unhappiness that has been happening since she was ten and which she has almost become inured to: "It has happened over a course of four years, gradually, like growing" (52). The "growing" metaphor implies the nuclear family and, in the bigger picture, the social family as site of growth. The family's sterility brings on such stunting experiences, which grow like weeds in what should be good garden soil if it was tended right. On this occasion, while the old man holds her so she cannot leave the barn they are in, and whispers, "Show me your tits . . . I'll give you a dollar if you do" (52), Betty finds consolation in the decision she has made that morning to tell on Mr. Joy at the Wednesday ladies' circle.

When she enters the circle that evening, her resolve fades. The ladies, with Betty listening and respectfully waiting her turn to "tell," discuss the sin of suicide in the context of a story of a thirteen-year-old Russian girl who has been repeatedly raped over a period of two weeks and who finally shoots herself. Betty's mother Mika suddenly and impulsively announces that suicide must be the unpardonable sin or else she herself would have done it long ago. One woman remonstrates over Mika's candidness; another, the white-haired one whom Betty has taken a liking to, says meaningfully that "[o]ccasionally . . . in this room, someone dares to speak the truth" (57). Betty slips out of the room unnoticed then. Her own bitterness at Mr. Joy's intrusion, as well as her eagerness to expose him, slip, together with herself, into the background. Whatever she felt was significant in her life, enough to make her one of the ladies, to warrant such a group confession, which would rally them in support around her and end her lonely confrontations with Mr. Joy, their larger and more terrible secrets silence her, secrets which they keep to themselves, and which if they could reveal would cause them all to choose death over continued living. Consequently, because of some terrible duty, they go on hypocritically miming the life of joy themselves:

> The stone is back in her [Betty's] stomach. She feels betrayed. For a moment the women are lost inside their own thoughts and they don't notice as she rises from her chair and sidles over to the door. Then, as if on some signal, their conversation resumes its usual level, each one waiting impatiently for the other to be finished so they can speak their words. Their laughter and goodwill have a feeling of urgency, of desperation. Betty stands at the door; a backward glance and she sees the white-haired woman bending over her work once again, eyes blinking rapidly, her fingers moving swiftly and the doily, its flecked pattern spreading like a web across her lap. (57)

"Like a web across her lap" the doily stretches. Domestic work, forgetting work, busy work, various sorts of "nets" to catch the thoughts and feelings and hold them back, keep emotions from spilling out because life is so terrible for women, the implication goes, that if they let down their guard they would die. Specifically, sex and touch, among the greatest pleasures the material world offers, are sealed off by the doily virginity belt. In a world where women wish to die but duty keeps them busy, blinking back tears while they work, who would wish to impose her own paltry worries on anyone with such a high quotient of suffering? Betty is the oldest of the Lafreniere girls. Each of the girls in her turn, as well as their mother, tells stories as deadening to desire as this.

In "The Rock Garden," a series of narrated events ends in Mika's sudden great annoyance with mothering. Lureen, watchful and precocious Lureen, notices Mika make a mysterious midnight trip away from the house and then hours later back to it, carrying a rock, which she adds to a growing pile under the children's swing. That starts the sense of mystery around the mother figure for both the reader and Lureen. Significantly, the reader draws closer to Mika, knowing she feels and desires, whereas the discovery of her mother's secret nighttime world distances Lureen from Mika. The members of the nuclear family wish for the end of the mother's desire, while the reader wishes for more of it. The family model as we know it, Birdsell seems to dramatize, stifles desire and love.

Lureen has been trained to expect loyalty and consistency and devotion from mothers, not pleasure and active, new, unpredictable living in the world. Where could she be going in the night when she should be asleep? we, as much as does Lureen, ask ourselves. The complication of the mother's life (Mika's in "The Flood," except now "the mother's" because seen from a daughter's perspective) here includes Lureen tattling on her sister Betty out of jealousy since she has been hanging around with Laurence, a vagabond family's son, who has eyes for none of the Lafreniere girls but Betty. Mika, angered over the information—the false information—from Lureen that Betty and Laurence have been necking in the coulee, dramatically declares Laurence off limits to Betty. Then, in exasperation at her husband and the children, she begins the endless task of building the mysterious stones into a rock garden. Questioned by Maurice about the reason for her sudden impulse to build the garden, she flares up at him and says she is tired of her life. Maurice reminds her that she should quit this impulsive work outside and go inside where she's needed, where the babies are lying in sopping diapers.

> Mother grunted as the wheelbarrow tilted suddenly from her grasp and fell onto its side. "Well, change them then," she said. "They're your babies too."
>
> "What's the matter?" he asked, lowering his voice. "Is it— are you in the family way?"
>
> Mother stopped shovelling and looked him straight in the eye. "Yes. I'm always in the family way. And I'm tired. I'm tired of being a mother." (74)

Lureen overhears and feels unable to reconcile this with what she understands of the dependability of mothers. She recognizes that "mother" is a relative term, though, and at the end of the story, after a series of special efforts by Betty and herself to lure Mika back inside the house, she begins to consciously separate herself from her mother in ways more desperate than normal:

> I knew my mother had some of the answers to the mysteries. But the pull of an alliance between sisters was stronger. It was better than being on your own with a person who could suddenly grow tired of being your mother.
>
> "Piss, shit and God," I said. "A mean witch." I stepped out and away from my mother. Suddenly, I was afraid. (78)

The connection of mother with witchery suggests the ordinary metaphor we use when we declare someone we have learned to dislike to be mean and unwelcome. It also suggests more. It hints at the supernatural, which hovers everywhere in the background of these stories, sometimes far in the background, at other times closer and specifically functioning in the dramatic lives of the characters.

In "The Flood," we saw it in the fortuitous answers to Maurice's prayers that the courthouse walls cave in to prove he is truly the town's "Old Man River" (14), and their fall vindicates Maurice, Aboriginal people, goodness, supernatural powers, all in one fell swoop. In "Truda," the girl by that name has been discouraged by an insensitive Mika from doing what she loves most, which is drawing. Underestimated and unappreciated by her family, Truda is shown by the narrator to have a wonderful kinship with the spirit of the land, a spirit that none of the other Lafrenieres even begin to imagine or respect. In a mysterious scene hearkening back to the biblical story of the flood and

Maurice's intuition, which helps him predict another flood, the artistic Truda sees a lake forming close by her, in this land the reader remembers as the not-so-dry remnants of the greatest freshwater lake ever, Lake Agassiz:

> Truda waited. She leaned into the fence and looked at the lake. It jumped forward and channels of water tipped down the highway towards her. It was all in her head but she could smell fish and see shells and sand. The gulls flew low, crossing and crisscrossing each other's flight paths. She could see their black feet tucked up against white-grey bottoms. She looked down and saw milky water receding before her feet, leaving wet crescent marks on the ends of her navy sneakers. (43)

Until here, the picture of the water seems all only imaginary. Then, however, the description begins to double back on itself, fold back the veil of image and introduce the drama of the real:

> Beige sand, dappled with curious flat grey pebbles, rounded perfectly smooth, was left in the water's wake. She stooped, picked several pebbles and dropped them into her pocket before the white frothy water rushed back up, cold, overtop her shoes and then up around her ankles. She lifted her eyes to the lake. The gulls cried with joy and bounced their solid bodies against the lake. It was like nothing she had ever drawn. (43)

The lake ebbing and flowing, the girl's clear seeing, and the cry of the gulls come to the reader as sensually immediate, as if Truda has been transported into another realm where the impossible may happen, where the past—the actual wave-lapping and shore action of Lake Agassiz—becomes present and living.

The mind's unconjured images conjure up a world of the real, which makes time irrelevant and threatens to disrupt the deep-rooted and impervious movements of history itself, so sure are we suddenly that the flood that came to Agassiz is somehow Truda's doing, somehow the doing of a child, somehow the doing of the artist. The flood, which historically came to the "Agassiz" region in the 1950s is the flood of *Night Travellers*; the flood of "The Flood" is the flood of a historic past but it is the flood of the general artist remembering the flood and giving it special, humano-cosmic significance. The flood of "The Flood" is the unsettling return of that greatest of the Great Lakes, which laps with mystic power at the backs of the prairie imagination, and the flood in "Truda" is the mysterious real overpowering the sad and ordinary unreal of the prairies and, specifically, the desiccated family relations that mis-operate in a world that (like that of T.S. Eliot's *The Waste Land*) has lost all power to live by the spirit.

To bring this picture back to the story's drama, the impression given is that Truda's experience with the rising lake is shamanistic, mystic. Truda, the artist, conventionally myopic and always underfoot in Mika's kitchen, possesses a gift that none of the others dream of, the gift of prophetic sight. Immediately on establishing the link between artist and vision, and so between her stories and the supernatural, the narrator brings the focus back to the issue that drives the book thematically:

> She didn't need crayons when she had all this in her head. Mika could never take away her head. Her own gull rose. She felt the cold water around her calves, at her knees and then it swirled about her thighs. She took a deep breath and dove under. She didn't need to draw the farm. The farm was gone and her imagination was a tree growing inside and green leaves unfolding one by one. (43)

I cannot help but notice the curious connection between Di Brandt's operant metaphor for the victim's imagination and this one of Birdsell's. Brandt describes her imagination thus, as a tended treeling:

> you come bearing gifts green apples
> glistening in a red bowl you have
> waited all your life for this moment
> tended your small tree carefully (*Agnes in the sky* 19)

Mika keeps the crayons from Truda. Truda needs them no more. Her mind, her ability to create the reality she wants in full colour and with all the sensations in place, makes her much more powerful than her prohibiting mother. Birdsell draws mothers coldly; a great distance grows between mothers and daughters. Mothers in Birdsell's world obviously do not know how to give the daughters what they need. This, again, is reminiscent of Brandt's poetry. Mothers once were, before Brandt's poetry, terribly hard on daughters. How, then, can daughters learn loving behaviour, both Brandt's and Birdsell's writing might be asking. What daughters need from mothers, the effect of Birdsell's writing leads us to understand, is to be led into a spiritual world in which the ordinary and the tedious do not dominate.

Birdsell's narratives inextricably link the extraordinary and the ordinary. The stories of *Night Travellers,* as well as those of the novels, reinforce this unbending relationship. The powerful, intriguing opening of "Night Travellers," the title story of the collection, perfectly demonstrates the conventional fiction of the extraordinary-ordinary in production.

> "When a woman has intercourse," Mika told herself, "she thinks of what might happen." She climbed in the night the hill that led away from the river and James. She travelled in a black and white landscape because it was void of details that would have demanded her attention. And the night was also a cover. Above, the starlit summer sky served only to make God seem more remote, withdrawn. (79)

Mika, as we know from the earlier stories, represents one version of the ordinary woman. She has cursed her husband's slothfulness and late nights' drinking, she has resented the work of raising children while her apparently kindly husband inquires what might be wrong, she has vilified the whole enterprise of watching the river and so vilified her husband with whom we as readers have grown sympathetic. In our eyes, she appears hard and mean, a "witch," as Lureen declares. Her actions here of climbing a hill in the night, thinking of the intercourse that she barely tolerates with Maurice, given her shrewish conduct towards him, of imagining the landscape to be black and white and "void of details," as well as the passing reference to a distant god summon up the quotidian much as would a story by Raymond Carver. Simultaneously, however, these very details here, all, every one, and a host of others I have not mentioned for brevity's sake, carry a weight of the marvellous with them. Why would a woman alone at night outdoors be thinking of intercourse? This unusual topic sets the "miraculous" tone, or at least the note of the unexpected, for succeeding details and for the entire story. Climbing the hill whispers both of glory and of tedium, God on his hill and Sisyphus on his (as well as "Mac Flecknoe," Satan at the opening of Book Two of *Paradise Lost*, the writer hacks in their Fleet Street ditch in Pope's *Dunciad*, David Canaan on his mountain in *The Mountain and the Valley*, and, of course, many others).

She climbs the allegorical hill of Difficulty and "mothering," and heads back down it again after a few fleeting hours with her secret lover, James. She heads away from the river, which here represents the miraculous if only Agassiz subjects would take note of it the way Truda has indirectly done and as Maurice himself describes, even though, when all is said and done, he does not follow his own fine instincts in this matter or really comprehend the extent to which his understanding of the river is both practical and quotidian, technical and miraculous:

> Maurice cleared his throat to speak. Build a sewage treatment plant so we no longer shit and piss on the river. We didn't have floods like this one until we got the running water. My God, the river, she doesn't pretend to be beautiful, but some honour is due, eh? Lure the goldeye and pickerel back with clean water. Forget the Indian legend that says we have no say in the matter. We should remember the river, she gave this region its life. But he knew they saw the river with different eyes. To them it was heavy, sluggish and ugly, a breeding ground for mosquitoes and eels. (12)

The river in the stories is potentially miraculous and ordinary, depending on how it is seen. Mika, walking away from the river, walks away from the shamanic and lovable Maurice and toward the one whom she despises. Walking away from James, from whose bed of "intercourse" she rises, she walks away in her imagination from a wonderful and charming contrast to her husband, but in the reader's eyes an ordinary and dull man who gives back to her the hairpins she (charmingly and shrewishly, both) leaves on his bed hoping to force him to remember her after she is gone.

This same extraordinary/ordinary vein climaxes in the story of her reunion with her father, who discovers her adultery and to whom she makes an unlikely, tearful promise not to return to James's bed. It ends with Mika's attaining what she thinks of as peace, now that the reconciliation with her Mennonite tradition represented by her father has taken place. She thinks she is at peace, but the imagery in the last lines of the story tells the reader otherwise.

> She turned her face against his [her father's] chest and stared into the night beyond him. She felt empty, barren, but at peace. In the garden, a bright glow flared suddenly and she thought, it's a cigarette. But the glow rose and fell among the vegetation and then became bead-shaped, blue, brighter, her desire riding the night up and up in a wide arc, soaring across the garden into the branches of thick trees. A firefly, Mika thought. And she watched it until it vanished. (89)

Significantly, and supporting my idea that in Birdsell's work the ordinary never recognizes the miraculous, Mika feels barren. All along she wishes not to have more children, if she wishes for children at all. To resist bearing children constitutes a highly deterritorializing desire on her part, the nadir of desire, desire's absence, really. Mennonites, and Aboriginal people too, are traditionally known for their huge families. Mika forecloses on this tradition and replaces it with nothing except a desire for barrenness, which is to say, a desire for the alienation out of which the characters Birdsell generates, both here and in future works, all construct themselves to excess. The firefly/cigarette, magic and mundane mixed in one metaphor, ride up and down in the night, as Mika has done with James. The garden it rides in, though, despite all the apparatus of allusion to that other religious garden we in the West know so well, will never produce much of anything. Mika has wished just that. Mika has, in the years of her growing up, been so stultified by the particular discourse of transcendence and barren desire of her father's tradition that she cannot think of a thing she would like as much as a peaceful barrenness.

Similarly, individualistic impulse blinded by circumstances and stupid wilfulness at the most critical moments characterizes how everyone except Minnie operates in Birdsell's first published novel, *The Missing Child*. Stupid wilfulness occurs there not as an oddity, but frequently, inevitably. Minnie comes from heaven. God, her tyrannical though beloved parent/lover, goes by the name of Jeremy. Mozart plays his wonderful new musical creations in heaven's garden while Minnie, bored with being chained in this heavenly, barren Eden for eternity, peeks down at the earth from the sky. Here, from the other side of the trees bordering the garden, she sees the valley and the people milling about down below. She longs to descend and participate in the excitement of human concourse. Finally, one day, when some event accidentally loosens her chain—she has been kept on a chain in heaven because of her unpredictability and impetuosity—she slides down into the valley and joins the human race to live there and to eventually warn it of approaching disaster. (I am reminded of Raphael's uninformed descent into Eden to warn an uxorious Adam not to serve the headstrong Eve.)

Her coming to earth in an earthly body parodies Christ's incarnation, of course, and her purpose, like His, culminates in her ultimate predictions of eschatological doom. The book both begins and ends, in fact, with this apocalyptic moment, the coming of a great, purging flood. Minnie, floating naked down the river through the valley, under a bridge on which sits a Bible-quoting boy looking salaciously down at her—she owns a lovely figure, we discover in the course of our reading—announces that the end has come for the valley. The valley, of course, fails to listen to her, the novel tells us at length, and eventually Minnie leaves the region, presumably for her old heavenly home, shortly before the flooding of the valley becomes a reality.

The mysterious and transcendent thematically dominate this book, as they do *Night Travellers*. Heaven, magic, mystery, spiritual possibility not sensed by the valley's individual subjects, anchor the narrative. Yet, no one notices mystery's presence nor has the ears to hear. Too busy and too wrapped up in their own severity, selfishness, plots to deceive and get ahead, and processes of personal dissolution, none take notice. Minnie extends to the Agassiz populace plenty of opportunity to hear her prophecies concerning the extra-normal, but, ignored and reviled, in the Messianic tradition, she is judged incompetent. This is a prophecy the narrator indicates right from the start of her story: "As Minnie Pullman floats on the river and sings, it's clear to her that the neat lines of the valley, the charted ancestries of families, ethnic backgrounds, languages, quaint customs are going to be wiped out. The glacier is melting and the river is rising" (6). Even her own believed her not. Her daughter Rosella despises her. Her other daughter, Ginny, loves and protects her even though she thinks her mother flighty and terribly eccentric. In an interesting glance at classical myths, Birdsell makes these two girls the daughters of a god. Minnie, goddess, generates Rosella and Ginny, who never come to know the man/god mix in their genetics. Usually in myth, such liaisons generate males who eventually discover their divine origins. Rosella and Ginny presumably will experience the catastrophe Minnie predicts and possibly die in it. Minnie is loved and hated both, but never understood or even properly listened to. Her message, one which she only indirectly gives and which she often realizes herself in a haphazard way, though never with much conviction, is that the valley as it has been will soon and catastrophically end.

Everywhere there are indications of apocalypse; nowhere is there any agitation over it because nowhere is there anyone, not even extraterrestrial Minnie most of the time, who possesses the power of spirit to hear, see, feel, or understand its immanence.

> It comes to Minnie then that she could try and warn them. She could ride a horse through the streets, down the wide centre of Main, past the Red and White store where in the window, blind, sun-faded mannequins shamelessly model Gothic cotton brassieres and where upstairs in a large unpainted room lined with caskets, Mr. Harrigan, the store proprietor, stands behind a purple curtain. He leans over a coffin and places sprigs of lily-of-the-valley between Sandra Adam's young fingers. (6)

Sandra's death indicates the great extent of Agassiz's social depravity, one that would seem to invite an apocalyptic end to life in the valley. Sandra Adam has been murdered by Sonny, a disreputable young man-about-town who gets away with the deed. Lily of the valley is, of course, the death flower and constitutes an eschatological symbol for the geographical valley at the moment its dissolution begins. The "purple curtain" behind which the simple local death-drama unfolds will soon be rent in twain. The town lives on and will do so oblivious till the end, weakly concerned with its death, sex, and security in, and sales of, clothes, caskets, sex and death.

Mr. Harrigan's actions, not unlike those of the adult lover in the old movie version of *Lolita*, place items between young Sandra's fingers. There is a suggestion of perverse love here, of necrophilia, of a complicity of the town in prohibited love of adults for female children. This subject enters a number of Birdsell's stories, and effectively makes of modern life a wasteland, sexually perverse, spiritually blind. The Lolita syndrome, with its waste and ignorance, lives here in this sleepy town, a town dead to the presence everywhere of death and signs of death, dead to its own mortality. All in this town is asleep, perverse, "lulled to death":

> Minnie might clutch a horse between her thighs and cry out as she rides, "Gather up your photo albums, your diaries, your histories of the valley and run for the hills." But they wouldn't listen. Her desire is lulled to death by the rocking motion of the river, by the inevitability of the rising water. She frog-kicks and glides forward swiftly and smoothly. She passes through the shadow of the steel bridge and feels the chill of its spanners cross her glistening belly. (6)

In her imagination Minnie is Lady Godiva riding naked through the streets of Coventry. The significant difference is that Coventry people did not *see* Godiva, who was doing them an enormous favour, interceding with her husband concerning taxes. Agassiz will not *listen* to the warning. It is the people here who have lost all reason for a visionary's or a benefactor's sympathy, and not a cruel tyrant deaf to the cries of his people, as in the Godiva story.

The bridge boy Hendrick speaks trenchantly, too, from these opening pages. He is the closest thing Agassiz has to a home-grown prophet, a totally inept and stupid one: "As she drifts through its shadow and out the other side, she sees the soles of Hendrick Schultz's boots as he sits on the top span swinging his legs back and forth. It's a lazy, hypnotic motion and if he should lean too far forward he would be carried away" (7). Despite his lack of coordination, which speaks of poorly developed large motor skills, and so of his baby qualities, he amazes the townspeople, who for the most part revere and fear him. Here he is seen spouting Bible verses from memory (significantly from the prophetic books of Zechariah and Daniel), peeping—not unlike the "peeping Tom" tailor in the Godiva story—down through the bridge grating at a naked woman, about to fall in the river and drown, in parodic foreshadowing of the way lovely Sandra Adam dies later. Prophecy in Agassiz, in other words, has no future. Only selfishness inheres. Where and in what novels have we not heard this before? Birdsell, however, writes this theme with great complexity and new humour and so contributes something valuable to the genre of modern alienation novels.

In the shadow of immanent presence, the entire story is told. Even when the writing goes on at length in a mundane way, without direct representation of a clear miraculous content in its world, underneath the unfolding of events, in the turn of a phrase, in its many quirks of decisions and oddities of natural phenomena (the new and growing artesian well in Agassiz; Jacob Friesen falling off Elizabeth's roof), the story is determined by the transcendental signifier. Albert's world, Sandra's world, June's, Jacob's, Elizabeth's, Robbin and Sonny's, Lena's, Ollie's, Steven Adam's, and Marie's worlds remain unconscious of immanence. These characters lack an understanding of presence. The most likely reason for their incomprehension is intellectual. Their stupidity is not only their fault, but somehow a natural flaw. Nature fails to provide for its citizens.

The inability to comprehend and a failure of communication dominate the relationship of Minnie and Annie Schmoon. Minnie comes from a heavenly world about which she babbles to Annie, who assumes she hallucinates. Annie's goodness and Dostoevskian moral superiority hit home to the reader in the way she continues to befriend Minnie despite her incoherence about Jeremy and Mozart. Annie's own life is miserable, considering her poverty, her frail health, and her affliction with cancer. She attempts to cure her cancer with home remedies, such as the consumption of frogs, which she spends much of her time catching and swallowing live.

Knowing the special status of Minnie as an angelic being, the reader smiles at her eccentricities. For this reason also, he finds it easy to accept the material world described by Birdsell at every stage of the story. The pain in the eyes, the newspapers lining the windows, the ratty toque, the steel wool hair, the weirdly patterned clothes on the line, and even the cancer growing in Annie all seem acceptable to the reader who knows that, according to the lyrical, romantic novel, a figure from another world represents the possibility of salvation of some sort.

> Her voice cracked and she turned, hawked, and spat. Minnie saw the string of blood in the mucus as it dropped to the grass. Annie wiped her mouth on the sleeve of her jacket. "Here," she said and stepped towards Minnie waving the clipping. A musty odour emanated from her clothing. Apples, Minnie thought. That Annie was an apple going soft inside. (16)

Lyrical convention assures the reader that some sort of spiritual vindication of the material lies in store for him. Annie may die in the end, he thinks, but she will not die for nothing. And in a way he guesses right. Minnie's very extraterrestrial existence means that desperation of individuals in this alienated world must be a perceptual problem. Humans simply do not see what is there for them to see. They fail to see. The cancerous blood, the mucus dropping to the grass, the wiping of the sleeve across the mouth, and even the apple smell of the old woman have a not entirely unpleasant ordinariness about them here for the reader. As the novel develops, however, with its endless failure of perception, its endless depiction of the material as abject in the eyes of its characters, the world which Birdsell creates for the reader turns gradually sour and hopeless.

Materials, things available to the body's senses, gradually lose all colour and warmth as we discover a variety of occurrences that, in their ordinariness, rob the body of joy. Sandra Adam is raped and murdered and her murderer, whose identity the reader ironically knows, will never be found or tried. Sonny, who murders her, is picked up by the RCMP for a damaged headlight and, though the reader knows he should be held for a more dreadful crime, she knows too that justice will not be served. Justice never is served anywhere in Birdsell's work, unless the serving of justice highlights some aspect of fallen hope, some travesty such a justice commits. Ollie loves Albert and has waited for fifteen years for him to love her as he used to, but despite a momentary return of a relationship between them, Albert lacks the strength of character to commit himself to her. Literary alienation convention determines that Ollie will live disappointed. Annie's home cure, mentioned to Minnie in the laundry-hanging scene, will not succeed, we know, and our expectations turn out to be accurate. On and on lumbers the litany of predictable death and growing disappointment. All desires that material bodies exercise on each other turn out unsatisfied. The absence of a visibly permanent relation of object and subject in the world of Agassiz leaves only one alternative to the disappointed narrator and author, the imagination of a world bereft of imagination, which is to say, a world empty of the gratification of desire. The material in Birdsell's work stands there in its mockery. It beckons us to try it, and then laughs at our efforts by wickedly whisking away what we have grown attached to. The opening scene with Minnie's bidding a confused good-bye to the world she once wished to inhabit, giving up on it, acts as the quintessential example of this attitude toward the material. God turns His back on Agassiz when Minnie leaves it. Desire gives up on Agassiz when Minnie leaves it. God gave up on Sodom after so many days and warnings.

Birdsell constructs worlds out of the ideological realm of morality, alienation, sentimentality, essentialism, and distrust of the material. The loss she represents in *The Missing Child*'s distress is epistemological loss. Stymied by the absence of knowable transcendence, she shows the reader transcendence emasculated and disappearing. Minnie leaving Agassiz is Robert Kroetsch's female, in his popular essay "Fear of Women," leaving the house and riding off on someone's horse, Godiva's horse, ironically, to be exact. Kroetsch says,

> The basic grammatical pair in the story-line (the energy-line) of prairie fiction is house: horse. To be *on* a horse is to move: motion into distance. To be *in* a house is to be fixed: a centring unto stasis. Horse is masculine. House is feminine. Horse: house. Masculine: feminine. On: in. Motion: stasis. A woman ain't supposed to move. Pleasure: duty. (*The Lovely Treachery of Words* 76)

If only the disappearance of Minnie Pullman represented the end of the old era of love of the absence of desire and the beginning of a new age when the material itself could sustain the interest of its bodies and subjects. The reader might almost find herself inclined to think this, given the title of the first chapter. Birdsell chooses, however, to write the extreme alienation of desire from its object.

Extreme alienation as moral regime based on a Platonic-Christian cosmology is clearly to be seen already in Birdsell's early stories, but with each successive book the intensity of the disappointment produced by the unsatisfying material is turned up a notch, until in *The Missing Child* and especially *The Chrome Suite,* it reaches its nadir. Where social material writing would find some disappointment and also some fulfillment of desires (which is what we call pleasure), anti-material writing (that is to say, lyrical, traditional, metaphysical, moralist, nihilist writing)—which seems to be, but only seems to be and is not, a pro-material writing because of its competence at verisimilitude—finds none. It shows characters never entirely failing to renew their hope for joy and union in this world and its social formations, but always failing to find even minimal satisfaction, unless that satisfaction is the hollow one of high spirituality, of the sort Margaret in *The Chrome Suite* hears when she listens to the old woman who preaches to her to be saved and so to atone for the sin that caused her daughter's death:

> "But my dear," Mrs. Hardy said, "won't you see that the Lord is calling out to you? He has taken Jilly to be with Him for a reason. Can't you see?" She stepped back and raised her face and hands and began to chant a prayer. At least I believe it was a prayer but I couldn't be certain because the words, though they sounded like words, didn't make any sense at all. When I left the house, Margaret's voice joined with hers and I heard my mother say, "Thank you, Jesus, for taking Jill away from me." (146)

The desperation in Margaret's and Mrs. Hardy's voices indicates a high degree of doubt about the efficacy of the meaning they have put in their faith. These religionists tell their Jesus what is real, the way a silly young boy babysitting for the first time might talk to his unhappy charge, whining, "Do you like these toys, hmm? Do you like these toys, hmm? You like these toys, don't you, yes, you do like these toys," all the while waving different objects he has grabbed out of the huge plastic toy box—trucks, duckies, plastic ninjas—an inch from the toddler's nose, who has begun to cry in the meantime, and whose crying only succeeds in making the foolish boy wave the toys harder, closer to the crying baby, and to speak his nonsense louder. They speak of Jesus the way Joe in D.H. Lawrence's "The Horse Dealer's Daughter" speaks to his dog when the loss of the family farm becomes fully clear to him:

> Joe watched with glazed hopeless eyes. The horses were almost like his own body to him. He felt he was done for now. Luckily he was engaged to a woman as old as himself, and therefore her father, who was steward of a neighbouring estate, would provide him with a job. He would marry and go into harness. His life was over, he would be a subject animal now.
>
> He turned uneasily aside, the retreating steps of the horses echoing in his ears. Then, with foolish restlessness, he reached for the scraps of bacon rind from the plates, and making a faint whistling sound, flung them to the terrier that lay against the fender. He watched the dog swallow them, waited till the creature looked into his eyes. Then a faint grin came on his face, and in a high, foolish voice he said:
>
> "You won't get much more bacon, shall you, you little b—?"
> (Lawrence 2586)

Joe does to the terrier what he imagines a whining, resourceless God has done to him, a God who grins with both a slight embarrassment at this discovery of his failure to provide, and a non-sharing, adolescent pleasure that He at least will not lose His job. Joe's God has the precise intelligence of Joe himself, or just a little less.

This absence of anything delightful in the material accosts the reader from the first pages of *The Chrome Suite* with Amy's separation from Pyotr. It continues through her story of her life. Her sister Jill dies an awkward and unnecessary death; her mother refuses to give her comfort despite a series of attempts on Amy's part to warm their relationship; Amy is raped by a psychotic who eventually kills Shirley Cutting, one of her only true friends; Amy's husband Hank spies on her and eventually begins to hate her; Amy's brother Mel comes for a few hours into the small town of Spectrail where she has been happily living for a few weeks and so soundly distracts her from her new sense of peace that she decides to leave Elaine and Laura, and late in the novel she loses her son Richard to Hank's custody. Finally, a series of apocalyptic events top off the novel: Pyotr is shot and killed by rebel Natives blockading a major highway; Amy takes time to let herself psychically experience her great sense of loss. Her loss is that lifelong procession of events that have bitterly disappointed her. She does not recover from these losses as the reader might expect her to do after a period of convalescence, now that Pyotr is dead. Instead, she adds to them. As a symbol of all the accumulated loss of everyone in the novel, and as a form of revenge taken by an injured lover, Amy ends the book with a final nihilistic act: she slowly burns all the journals and personal writings she had grown to count on to give her meaning, if normal things such as families, friends, and fine living could not. Page by page she burns her writings as Birdsell's account of her life comes to an end. The final words of *The Chrome Suite* combine alienation and transcendence in a parting blow at the material. The book ends with a wicked joke on Amy. "The swollen thing moves behind her rib bone, a slight sliding sideways, a pressure. A reminder" (364). Amy, like her sister Jill, will die of cancer. Jill died tragically from a kick in the groin by a vagrant bicyclist early in the novel. That episode generated almost all the succeeding events, which caused Amy's own alienation from home and friends. Like Jill, Amy, too, will die young, unfulfilled, and bitter. Nothing in this book simply happens without a vicious side effect, without an abundance of conventional, modernist meaning attached. As Nietzsche says, "Man would sooner have the void for his purpose than be void of purpose. . . ." (*Genealogy of Morals* 299). I bring in Nietzsche here, and his greatest insight, because, periodically throughout this book, I wish to indicate my surprise at the relentlessness of the human tendency to impose meanings on events. That relentless drive seems to me the most salient feature of even the writer's activities, even the writer's narrative purposes. Here we need to go to think about the future of writing. Here we need to go to create non-lyrically, to create the new.

Not only do these novels entrench the alienation/mysticism

dichotomy evident in Birdsell's earlier fiction, they intensify it as if the author had come to a gradually more intense certainty about her initial impulse, her beginning instincts about the empty universe and the *need* for something to fill it, but as if, convinced by her own early writing of this universal understanding, she increasingly lost faith in possibilities and found herself forced, for professional and personal reasons, to eliminate ever more fiercely any narrative possibility for earthly joy, earthly friendship, earthly and homey pleasure that spanned time. Her narrative violates all possibilities of progress, positivism, hope, growth or other indications of the teleological. It does not accept the absence of transcendent meaning but bitterly represents, by the objective correlative of various characterizations and plots, an intense picture of the moment of loss. That is, Birdsell does not show us transcendence lost and then forgotten about. That would mean a fiction of creative construction about what remains when transcendence no longer has any place in time and space. Birdsell dwells on the static moment of the discovery of loss as if that moment truly offered something significant and worthy of humankind's memory. In effect, Birdsell memorializes transcendence by showing the extreme emptiness of the human and natural landscapes that result from that absence. To memorialize is to erect a memorial to an event that then can be conveniently forgotten about because so familiar. To memorialize frees all to not think. Jean François Lyotard theorizes this human tendency to disremember (recalling Heidegger's view of the connection between memory, thanks and thinking): "But as far as forgetting is concerned, this memory of the memorial is intensely selective; it requires the forgetting of that which may question the community and its legitimacy" (*Heidegger and "the jews"* 7). Birdsell's narrative landscapes leave the print of violence toward teleology at every moment of the plot, at every stage in the development of character, at each contribution to the thematic intentions of the narrative, and at each establishment of setting and atmosphere.

7.

Writing Surplus: Recent Mennonite Writing

From the long list of active Mennonite Canadian writers, a few will receive attention in the following chapters. They have done much by way of poetry and fiction to make the politics of Mennonite Canadians known in ways that show persistence and expertise at asking what it means to be a Mennonite subject in the Canadian social landscape.

Lois Braun's books of short stories analyze the problem of the non-Mennonite Mennonite. They present essential selves who would like to be full members of the Mennonite community in which they move and operate. Products of eccentric homes, unusually gifted imaginations, and perceptive minds, these characters fit nowhere. Typically, the bizarre, the obtuse, the mysterious, or the dark attracts them. As in the writings of the early nineteenth century, destiny determines Braun's plots as well as her characters and the events they endure. In the Romantic tradition, Braun prefers certain character types: children, outcasts, rural eccentrics, the impoverished, and utterly solitary figures. Braun's protagonists desire to escape from what in each story seems to be some sort of great restriction. The subject in each story imagines itself to be a nomadic subject free to cross over various social boundaries that effectively bind it.

Braun's characters escape men. She treats women lovingly, lustily, while men receive negative sexual attention. Women physically and psychically interest the narrator; men do not. Take the description of Darcy in "Between Moon and Flax Fires" as she discusses her birth-mother with Claire: "Darcy stretches out her legs in front of her, legs in dark green leotards, and winds a white undershirt around her feet" (*The Pumpkin-Eaters* 246). The emphasis on legs and what colourfully covers them is obvious. The way Darcy plays with her legs entices Claire to be interested in them. A slightly more restrained description in the story of a kind female police officer suggests a connection for Claire between daughter and constable, who sits down beside her in the dark and whom the narrator cautiously describes as "stretch[ing] her legs out in front of her" (256). This may seem minor, but men are not similarly physically described.

Loving, colourful, sometimes seductive descriptions of females are found in her latest collection, *The Montreal Cats,* in stories such as "Toxic Wastes." Here, two rather witless beauties find themselves at the garbage dump on a Sunday, illegally disposing of "toxic waste" hair conditioner, which they have been sold in bulk. The descriptions seduce: "One of the women—the blonde one with the wide mouth and full lips—slid off the hood of the station wagon and came towards them" (20); "Suzy and Loretta made faces at Dale and Otto and waved both hands, which sparkled with rings and bracelets" (22); "but Loretta went to the driver's door of the station wagon and reached in with her long pink fingernails. She stuck her arm in up to her shoulder, and when she withdrew it, rock-and-roll followed. Breezes peppered with ash and smoke lifted her heavy blonde hair and the sun reflected off her glossy mouth" (24-25). The lusty gaze at the female by the author/narrator suggests a special narrative interest in the female sexual body, although oddly only in the fashionable body, not the one with sexual functions. Women loving women would surprise no one, except that these stories are told within the context of Mennonite Canadian territory.

In "Tatoo," the female narrator, despite her announced disapproval of Natalie, who, it turns out, has abandoned her husband and one of her children because of a problem with alcohol, is sexually drawn to Natalie at the same time.

> Ingrid had only been able to stare at the lusty, handsome woman who was her sister, but was so unlike her, Ingrid. She stared at the copper loops and rings and bands Natalie wore in her ears, on her arms, her fingers, and at her copper-coloured hair, and at the white sweatshirt with the ragged armholes where the sleeves had been cut away, and at the copper-coloured tendrils peeking out from Natalie's underarms. (39)

The narrator empathizes with women leaving their husbands. Even though Natalie left because of *her* drinking problem, the leap from thinking of her as a sorry excuse for a mother, to thinking of her as the victim of a lifestyle unsuited to her flamboyant and mysterious character, is a short one. The narrator lacks the stomach to escape from a domestic contract except via extraordinary means (means which underline the frustration that staying in the contract signifies). The above description captures as well as can be the irresistible aura of Natalie for the narrator. She takes on a sublimity of character, a weirdness, an eccentricity that removes her from the mundane world inhabited by the narrator. Natalie is a Romantic character: an individual, "dark," remote, ragged, rough, disorderly, nonconformist. Rings cover her fingers ("rings on her fingers, bells on her toes, she shall have music wherever she goes"), rings not made of gold (gold being too common an uncommon metal), but of copper: bright, gleaming, startling copper with which her copper-tanned body glistens.

Females not only get along better with women than with men, but they also appear more attractive in body and mind than their male partners. In "The Laughter of Women," for instance, Rea Jean discovers that her sister has slept with her husband-to-be. The upshot of the story, after much fear within and disruption to family relations, is that the sisters touch, comfort, and laugh with each other in a world without men. "And above, in the kitchen, amidst the banging of cupboards and the filling of pots, could be heard the rising and falling of voices, the laughter of women" (*The Montreal Cats* 104). Shutting men out as well as implying women's sexual preference for other women is a new form of textuality in Mennonite Canadian social politics.

In "Hunting Clouds," we meet a female narrator who has recently encountered a young and handsome German youth.

"Luther had sort of a breathless way of talking and permanent-ly messy dark hair and a smile that knocked your socks off" (*A Stone Watermelon* 175). To any heterosexual female in English literature, this man would typically be considered a "catch." The moment the narrator describes him, however, she intro-duces into the plot the death of "the Cat." At first this incident seems innocuous, but gradually it takes on significance. All that happens in "Hunting Clouds" is told, and needs to be under-stood, against the background of the dramatic tension between the handsome man and Cat ("Cat" is this particular feline's name, and so stands for everycat—this cat's significance as the story plays it out will have significance for the narrator's entire world). In the first place, Luther himself discovers Cat. If Cat were *his* best friend, it would seem plain that he was dying to the narrator since the narrator has an odd fixation in this story with this particular animal, and elsewhere with cats generally. Braun's female characters tend to favour cats, her male ones dogs. Cat was *Natalie's* favourite. The importance of these facts strikes the reader only gradually as the story develops.

A woman on a midnight boat ride with a young man, accord-ing to literary dating codes, must be starting to be enticed and to fall in love with him, as well as tempting him to fall in love with her. This story subverts that major heterosexual literary conven-tion. The narrator almost immediately gets annoyed with the prospective lover.

> And then this morning, while standing in front of the cot-tage, listening for the loon, Luther found the Cat. Dead and under the veranda. I was annoyed that an exchange student from Germany should have to find a dead cat under his host's veranda, but even more, I felt bad about the Cat. It had been difficult enough to come back here. (175-176)

Why has it been so difficult for her to "come back here"? It had been difficult because it was Natalie's favourite cat, and after Natalie died, Cat's spirit died, too.

When it comes to writing style, Braun can string together ordinary, colourless, lethargic verbs with the best of them: "went," "is," "was," "sat," and so on. Suddenly, however, the moment she introduces cats, her verbs jump with energy.

> She'd been lurking around Bruno's for years. She didn't belong to him, though, but roamed the lakefront from cottage to cottage, birthing kittens, resisting affection, hunting mice, eating barbecued steak bones and corn-on-the-cob and ends of wieners. She always turned up at wiener roasts. First, you'd see her spotty yellow eyes glowing in the poison ivy patch, then her whole body slinking nearer as the wiener ends began to plop in the grass. I'd known the Cat for as long as I'd been coming to Bruno's cottage at the lake, but Natalie had been the only one who could get near her. (176)

This cat lurks, slinks, births, resists, eats steak bones, hunts mice, and so forth. Significantly, since if the narrator is herself hunting "mice" (here a possible pseudonym for hunting females and likely a euphemism for female genitalia), then hers is a form of hunting clouds, or of hunting for what cannot be had or touched or experienced here on earth for anyone as *practical* and territorial as the narrators of Braun's stories. Eating in literature is typically sexual. There is a freedom of desire in this eating/hunting scene rare in Braun's work. Furthermore, cats have a romantic value for Braun, not to be found in humans. Cat here, more than her German friend, acts as the nomad cat, the alter-ego cat, the *real* object of the narrator's affections. "I could not eat, hadn't all day. Everything had been fine yesterday, comfortable and familiar. But this morning, Natalie's not being here and finding the Cat dead had twisted my stomach into a knot" (176). When we finally encounter a dead cat in Braun's fiction—her stories teem with cats befriended by women and hated by men—it is the dead cat of a woman whom the narrator obviously loved. Her nausea long after her friend's death indicates her deep affection. So does her specific awareness of Natalie's presence and moods before Natalie's death, a time to which the narrator now returns. Natalie's husband, gone fishing in bad weather one day, fails to come back. Reluctantly, everyone admits that he has had an accident. The likelihood crushes Natalie:

> "Finally Natalie just stayed on the dock. She sent me away. It was cold that night, and I brought her a blanket. I remember how she just sat there, huddled under that white blanket

in the moonlight. I'd go out to her, to try to get her in the cottage, but she was frozen to that dock. She didn't say anything, just wouldn't let me touch her. (177)

She thinks only of the woman, not of the poor man just now drowned. She concerns herself with this woman's bodily needs, and her coldness, significantly. Literally huddled under a blanket, Natalie might also be conceived of by the narrator as "cold" or "frozen" because she is preoccupied only with a man and the loss of him. The "frozen" serves a double purpose here. Much as in Milton's *Comus*, where the sister, in the masque she watches, is suddenly "frozen" to the spot, obviously from sexual juices that naturally embarrass her, Natalie is frozen, too. In the narrator's imagination, that freezing is possibly because the death of a man who controls the affections of the woman *she* would like to have under her control, fills her with an unnamable delight or pleasure. The pleasure might be as simple as the freeing up of her "lover," with her husband's death, from a contract to which the "lover" has been socially bound. Her pleasure might be more complex, a more murderous "hunting" instinct that experiences arousal (and imputation of arousal) in the news of the death of a male adversary.

Whatever the case with the concern over warmth and cold, Natalie will not allow the narrator to touch her. This seems to be an odd incident for her to recall here on her boat ride with a young, handsome man, unless some significance is attached to that fact. Just at the moment when the narrator tells of her great loss when Natalie goes insane, the boat bumps into a watermelon floating on the lake. In a scene pumping with sexuality, they eat the watermelon in the dark while reminiscing about Natalie. The eating becomes both a description of and a killing of the narrator's desire for the woman. The watermelon symbolizes the unconsummated, forbidden relationship between the two. Interestingly, it is the male Luther who "slashes."

> "Do you think it is safe to eat?" he asked. I could hear his knife slash into the melon and the juicy splitting of the flesh.
> "Yes, I'm sure it is. I'm hungry."
> "Turn around."
> He'd cut the fruit in half. The melon was small, probably homegrown. With his Swiss Army knife, Luther carved out

crisp wedges and handed them to me on the blade. "How did she die"? (180)

Notice the peculiar concern with safety, the salacious and violent slashing of the fruit/Natalie with the knife, the specifying of the fruit as flesh, the sexual implications of both the narrator's declaration of hunger and the bedroom language of the command that she "turn around." The cutting of the "crisp" flesh and the idea of Natalie are both present in the carving, and then immediately there is the interest in the mode of her death. "Crisp," moreover, usually connotes something young and delectable, something in clothing or in materials of various sorts that make them desirable.

> "It is not usual to lose your mind when your husband dies."
> "No. It was just something about Natalie. But—it's made me afraid. Afraid that a loss of someone I love will make me insane, like her. We were sisters. How much like her am I?" (180)

She *is* different from the woman she loved, that is precisely the point the narrator wishes to write into her story of her friend's death, one that she cannot and would not divulge directly. Luther must only know her distinctness indirectly, not that he will ever understand, but that way the narrator forestalls going insane. By hinting frequently at her forbidden love for Natalie (and other women, in consequence), the narrator preserves her equilibrium.

> "But you already have the answer. You are not like her. The Cat never went to you, did it? And you have lost someone you loved—Natalie. And here you are, still sane, yes?"
> "I don't know. I suppose I am. Insane things happen around me. Like finding this watermelon in the lake. Maybe this is what becomes of cats when they're buried at sea. Perhaps this is where I should have buried Natalie." (180)

This story—and writing, living—is for Braun's narrators all about burying Natalie. Here the homoerotics are covered over with an almost convincing coding of sibling love. She is sane, yes, but not as the major, territorial Mennonite Canadian world is sane.

Braun's challenge to Mennonite territory (which is a form of the major) works in this way. If not for the eating of the watermelon, the high sexuality of this story would not be as plain and defensible as it is. But this story, and others Braun writes, establishes the impossibility, given Mennonite Canadian politics, of loving as you desire. Subterfuge among them abides in all forms of love and desire. Officially sanctioned, pleasure must be couched and expressed textually, secretly, if at all. Territory jails. The narrator herself experiences ambiguity about the object of her desire. She projects onto Luther the appetite she has for Natalie. This sexual act—territorially appropriate on the surface of the text because well hidden and secretive, because heterosexual—lays to rest more than it arouses. Importantly for this story of misnamed love, Luther is German. He is aggressive and not submissive (not a cat); he slashes and carves the "sex" or flesh that the narrator then eats. He is not the intended lover but a ruse. The cat, nomadic, wandering like a waif, a lorn lover, loves Natalie. In loving Natalie it safely dramatizes the narrator's love for Natalie, a narrator who, in many of Braun's stories, persistently loves and derives excitement from cats.

John Weier is the second "recent" Mennonite Canadian writer I have chosen for this chapter. His narrative voice sounds naive and nonresistant to Mennonite Canadian codes. It appears uncertain of the conventions of major literature and so writes from a position of weakness with these lyrical conventions while *thinking* it is strong with them. The opposite is true. His understanding of the lyrical allows him to subvert major English literature effectively. Obviously, then, his assault on territory attacks the lyrical and the major rather than only Mennonite Canadian territory.

Weier's novel, *Steppe*, exemplifies his method very well for my purposes. The aim of the novel is historical. It reconstructs the Mennonite Russian past of the Mennonite Canadian group to which he belongs with ambivalence.

> A shoestring of stories about Russia, Ukraine. Where do they come from? Whose stories are they? Stories about peasants

and sailors and poets. What do they mean? How do they all fit together? Years. Kilometres. Dimensions. So far away. Beginnings? Where does it all start? Where are the books, the storytellers? I need to find out more about Russia. (1.5)

Weier opts to use a section/page notation to indicate place in the text instead of regular pagination. The page with the fifth entry in chapter two is marked 2.5, for instance. In postmodern style, with its subversion of orderly progression, Weier's text consists of a whole series of loosely connected, patternless fragments. Only late in the novel do the fragments become a story. He begins by giving us such diverse headings (and each page has a new heading above the entry for that page) as "Journal: September 3, 1992," "Father Remembers," "The Legend of the Foolish Peasant," "Mennonites, and Other Freethinkers," "Father: Longing," "The Apple Tree," "Mother: Bad Things," and "Katherine the Great." These appear to be the memories of individuals living today. Eventually, Weier adds some important characters who also keep diaries and write stories and who are clearly people from a previous age, contemporaries of eighteenth and nineteenth century Russian Mennonites. The narrative method is to eventually build a picture of the past based on a confusion of activity in the present. The author makes his method visible. He does not distance himself from his work. There are no pretensions to mastery or control. The storyteller obviously controls his text, but the message he presents is that he is not interested in hiding his control behind a self-effacing lyricism that pretends the perceived object is the only thing of interest to the reader and author both. This author cares enough about his subject to let everyone know how foolish and vulnerable he himself has frequently felt in his attempts to write the text before him now.

This same unpretentiousness characterizes Weier's choice of details and his method of presentation in *Steppe* in books such as *Ride the Blue Roan* and *After the Revolution*. In *Steppe* he tells with disarming simplicity and strong effect what he thought people back then in Russia and later, during and after their emigration from there, must have felt, thought, and done. He remembers his father's stories about his grandfather. The details are sparse; they barely do to let us know about the relationship between these two men. And we get very little else later to flesh the relationship out.

> (These are the things his father taught him. All these sound things . . .)

> Father pulls a blade of grass from the ground, stretches it between his thumbs and shows me how to blow through to make a whistle. It's a sharp sound, almost like a goat, always turns down at the end. Who knows where he learned this, perhaps from his older brother. (1.9)

The most significant quality of this metaphor for family relations is its naïveté. Everyone knows that old black and white movies show activities such as fathers teaching their children grass-whistle making, most farm kids had fathers, uncles or grandfathers love them by teaching them grass whistling, and so on. The young one cannot make a whistle. The old one has to show him many times before the little nipper somehow, mysteriously, begins to master it. The young one works and watches, works and watches, until after the twentieth time he gets a little squeak out of his blade of grass and the older one pats him on the back. The metaphor lacks something, common as it is. A writer would not typically choose to use it. Weier does.

> Whistles. Father cuts a little piece of willow branch, maybe eight inches, not too thick. He makes a few cuts in the bark and dips it into a pail of water. Twists. The bark slides off easily. A few notches, the bark goes back on. Here, father says, he puts the willow to his mouth and he gives a loud whistle. This one he learned from old Ivan the Russian, Ivan who lived and worked with the horses in the barn when father was little. (1.9)

Weier's use of the whistle-making story is sophisticated for two reasons at least: one, that it brings up the other elements of this history for the author as if it were the sheer simplicity of the memory of natural whistles that allowed him to get in touch with what he knows was a simpler age, a material age, an age when people suffered smaller tensions, conflicts, and difficulties with love. Yet the very simplicity of these tensions, as Mennonites wish at times to assert concerning their Russian territory, at the same time presents itself, as we have yet to see, as violent and destructive. The simplicity achieves dramatic effect by contrast and by the juxtaposition of the romantic with the violent quotidian.

Weier's treatment of the quotidian is sophisticated, too, in that it allows us to return to the material territory easily, neatly, leaving behind a late-twentieth-century sense of irony that, if present, would cancel the effect Weier has in mind of showing us people who believed they were simple, agrarian folk. We readers feel almost superior to the author himself. *We* would choose more complex lyrical (ironic) strategies, we say. By treating the reader so casually and nostalgically, however, Weier has him enter disarmed and receptive, and also romantically hopeful, into Mennonite territory. Despite our initial narrative expectations, *Steppe*'s Mennonite territory is in reality in the throes of a terrible deterritorialization as a result, among other things, of the Makhno Peasant Revolution of the early twentieth century. We discover that Makhno and his peasant army of forty thousand strong attacked Mennonite villages and burned them, briefly tried and summarily executed Mennonite men and women who resisted the peasant leaders' demands, and claimed as their own all property that belonged to Mennonites. This involved, violent story of peasant retaliation and Mennonite anti-pacifist resistance, which we have not expected, considering the naïveté of the metaphors, eventually emerges from *Steppe*'s fragments, but only gradually.

Weier is a more material writer than any of the others I have analyzed. He speaks for the people and its community, he cannot help but be political the moment he picks up his pen, and his language is packed with deterritorializing English language strategies, deterritorializing because English does not suit his Russian German subject. Listen to the "anorexic" English in this passage:

> You, poor man, you can't do anything else but you can teach.
> Here, this is a book. Can you spell it? B-o-o-k. That's good.
> See that shack? That's the school, the children are waiting
> inside.

Father was a good teacher. I'd like to teach. I like the children.
I like books. I like paper, the sound of pen on paper. I'd teach
them to read, to read and read and read.

I am only a woman. We are as poor as the Little Russians.
Listen, do you hear the wind? (2.2)

The woman whom Weier evokes in the passage might as well be
Weier himself. The love of children, the preoccupation with
father, the longing for and hope in books, and pen, and paper,
the narrative of "the Little Russians," which *Steppe* is engaged
with, are all precisely Weier's interests as well as any character's in
his stories. Furthermore—and here is the anorexic, sober connection—the language barely knows English.

Clearly, Weier is perfectly capable in lyrical English, in
major English. He chooses, however, to write in the unpreten-
tious style of the literary group he represents. His reasons for
reducing his language, his lyrical input, are comprised of a
combination of desire to write out of his setting, not out of an
imagined literary one established by the British over the last
thousand years, as well as out of a desire to love what is here.
For into all lyrical literature is written a hatred of the material
as Plato and Judeo-Christianity have taught. Weier loves food,
drink, sex, salaciousness, and all the body's various affects. He
has simple tastes, and certainly enough exuberance to embrace
both the too-wide world of spiritual disappointment as well as
the great, huge world of material pleasure. He chooses to write
within the old culture and its minor codings, using the material
tools of that culture, only mildly resisting that culture, and
then subverting the lyrical by a process of simple statement and
supra-clear—that is to say, anorexic, non-lyrical—English prose.

Sarah Klassen, too, writes simply, with a clearly territorial,
minor use of English, an English accustomed to speaking Low
German. She has published many books of poetry and all give a
similar impression of what it means to be a Mennonite Canadian
subject. They tell us that there is a Mennonite territory, and this
Mennonite territory must be poetized and written with love and
belief in order to preserve it.

Believers in territory are the bread and butter of good local
writing. They do not think that there is anything wrong except

the too-rapid deterritorialization of the world they love. To prevent disintegration of the community's codes, they find new ways to present the territory as they see it, as a form of asserting its permanence and power.

Unlike John Weier's, Sarah Klassen's poetry is about impossibilities. It narrates the story of lost territory and hopeless deterritorialization. In short, Klassen's work, lyrically patterned and colourful as it is, and not unlike Sandra Birdsell's sensibility of alienation, tells the reader about loss of hope. She is, in other words, a once young and hopeful one now, sadly, exhausted and wiser. She sees clearly what the young one only suspects but has not, unlike herself, graciously grown old enough nor disillusioned enough yet (though with grace and goodness) to understand. Youth does not yet understand the Neoplatonic relation between transcendence and beauty here on this earth, with youth's beauty a sign of goodness elsewhere in the universe, a goodness we humans have forgotten how to see. We have become too blinded by depravity and selfishness and sexual-sensual materiality to be able to see well. In brief, Klassen's narrator is modernist, lyrical, and believing thus in an alienated material universe, a depraved materialist universe. She turns always nostalgically toward the past to find examples of a naive hope and faith in which twentieth century consciousness, alas, no longer believes. It knows too much to believe. Klassen creates narrators who want to believe, who give every sign of being willing to believe if only the proof for belief existed somewhere, but who in the meantime in lieu of belief write poems warning the less wise younger ones (students related to by a teacher) that one day they too will see how much this teacher has really experienced, and will then see past her quiet, plain demeanour and recognize her wisdom and gutsiness about alienation. That is to say, Klassen believes in alienation and so, fiercely, in the transcendent. No hope for joy here. No love of sex, mouth, legs, food, and travel for their own sake, regardless of what she might long for, what she lacks and what is not to be had (according to the lyrical) even in the smallest portions here on earth. Only heaven can ever really suffice. The writing of poetry itself, and so the whole poetic enterprise, has for the lyrical tradition been the apex of the expression in the human world of the futile, though lovely, attempt to obtain what is unobtainable. Lyrical poetry such as Klassen's is thus, in its basic functioning, desire as lack: it is both the medium and the message of desire as lack.

"Black and White," a lovely poem about a new pupil who writes poems, which the teacher/poet reads with delight, tell sin little of this large "alienation-belief" disposition. First, it can be said that the narrator herself (as we have already seen in Braun's work) obviously hungers for the young, pretty, eccentric, lively girl who is the subject of the poem:

> porcelain skin. Most of it's covered with black
> leather and cloth, a sort of buffer
> against the possible onslaught of colour.

> Her skin shines like silver dollars
> through deliberate hole in black stockings.
> One of them's gotten out of hand.
> She's trying to hold it together
> with metal safety pins. (*Violence and Mercy* 9)

The narrator desires what (in a homophobic, youth-revering, politically correct, only partially urbanized age) a middle-aged woman feels she cannot have. She *can* have these things, of course, if she wants them, but the position of *wanting without being able to have them* is a conventional position lyrical territory—major literature—always takes, having been so successfully trained in, and itself the trainer for, the world view of desire as lack.

Nothing is *really* lacking for anyone in the world. It is conventional to write of lack. Klassen whispers to us in this poem about whispers, about secrets barely told, scarcely audible, that she can hardly stand something about this meeting with the "black" girl. What exactly can she hardly stand? Is it the violence behind the black on white motif of this girl's clothing? Is it a general violence against women and a repression of women of which this girl's dress and attitude strongly speak? Is it the great sensitivity, poetic and "elegant," of this Madonna who writes violence without understanding it yet? Such a violence, an acquaintance with loss, the poet herself ironically understands and knows that this girl will too understand some day. What the material tells us is that Klassen's narrator can hardly stand her own desire. But, for territorial reasons, she cannot admit that. She calls her desire something else—she calls it lack.

The narrator whispers secretively that she hungers for this girl. She wishes sexual, material, social, and psychic relations with her, but feels social prohibitions too strongly to say so.

> She prefers to sit near the back
> away from the window. She tells me this
> with lowered eyes, in thin whispers
> that almost get lost in the chalk dust.
>
> In order to tear my eyes
> from her black lips, black hair
> her matte black fingernails
> I study her poems. I'm not surprised
> she's mingled images of bleeding children
> with rats and black rain. (9)

"Black lips" and "black hair" and "matte black fingernails" draw our attention away from material desire to poetic convention. Hers is apparently a fashion problem and also a problem with violence. This is what all these black things give the reader the chance to think and so he does. That would be to think the "proper." The narrator, desiring the pretty, hurt, in-need-of-comfort-and-love young thing, desires her in a deterritorializing way, which at the same time seems to leave Mennonite and lyrical territory undisturbed.

> But I'm shocked at the sheer elegance
> of her calligraphy.
> Fear inked in delicate black
> whispers across the white page. (9)

This poem is all about black and white. Good and bad; proper and improper; love and lust. What fear haunts the girl? What fear haunts the older woman poet? The shocking thing for the speaker is the girl's "sheer" elegance; the girl's sheer "elegance"; the "delicate black," which "whispers across the white page." These tactile-auditory images derive from lingerie discourse. Delicate nylon things, underclothes, panties, slips and such other fineries worn next to the skin, whisper and float and cause fear in those who long for an experience with them. This sense of the erotic here in this poem generally between teacher and student, older woman and younger girl, inflicts a lovely violence on the reader's expectations of information reaffirming the time-honoured master narrative of the helpful matron and the hurt little girl, of grandmother and Little Red Riding Hood.

"Speeding" re-establishes a familiar, lyrical, spiritual territory. The poem describes a poet/writer whose car spins out of control on a frosty road and brings her close to death and so close to a classic moment of epiphany.

> Words tumble
> with the fearful speed of truth
> to the empty page. Pen
> clenched fingers, brain
> racing to get it right.
> Your nerves revved
> as if a revelation burns inside you
> or a still voice. (14)

The holy "still, small voice" of the biblical Pentateuch (I Kings 19:12) makes this poem of dying transcendent, otherworldly, suggestive of realms unknown to earthlings, though sometimes inspiring to us despite our usual dullness and unreceptivity. She continues with a now more earthly, more twentieth century image of God, less classical and outmoded than "still voice."

> I watch the sun
> reach for you with coy fingers. Instantly
> the innocent strands of your hair
> catch fire. (14)

The sun (commonly in lyrical poetry, and as I have shown it operating in Pat Friesen's *The Shunning*) here takes us "alienated" modern ones—afflicted by a sensual blockage seriously limiting our receptivity to a spirit there to be had in greater fullness in another, more glorious age—into the realm of the otherworldly, into bright, intensely lit non-material space. "Coy" and "innocent" bring in sex; "catch fire" removes the verse with its "intimations" of material love from the site of the material into the glorious realm where things have great meaning and possibility for satisfaction.

As in all her poetry, Klassen speaks for the territorial. She *hints* at pleasure on earth, but always takes that pleasure, for propriety's sake, into a non-territory, into the sky where the sun debacterializes it, where "a still voice" decontaminates it of its earthly dross. Social materialist, Klassen is not; territorial speaker for Canadian Mennonite values, she is. Take, for instance, "Wingspan," which appears toward the end of *Violence and Mercy.*

Remember the bird mother
coming to you in your cradle
was a vulture, not a swan.

When she fanned out her tail feathers
beat them against your small mouth
remember how you cringed

and cried out? Those grave wings
covered you like a judgement
carved out a nesting place

in your mind. How you examined
and reexamined them,
Leonardo. All your life

this obsession with birdwings.
The way they catch the updrift
of air, the mystery

of their conjunction with the body.
Each small muscle tendon bone
etched in your brain

and in your notebook. Larks
you set free in the marketplace
twittering to the sky.

You never wavered
from the stubborn airborne dream
that pinioned you:

one day your flesh would grow light

175

grow feathered wings
and from the summit of Swan Mountain

you'd fling yourself
and like an air-drawn eagle
fly. (96-97)

Leonardo knows something we today, hundreds of years later, have forgotten how to know. He had a faith in his world of wings. Wings, of course, stand for heaven, sky, the place of judgement and the source of love as the Bible and other classic texts teach. The artist, Leonardo, once sought with lifelong commitment to fly to the heaven he believed in with such admirable certainty. We, of course, the narrator tells us, can only admire the artists who themselves once believed thus fervently. We cannot believe that we will some day "fly," but we can remember and long for what we lack; we can long for a faith none of us are strong enough to possess.

Now, central to this poem, however, is a faith as strong as or stronger than the one Klassen attributes to da Vinci, the belief in the depravity of materials and the purity and "wing-like" refinement of that world from which we are alienated in knowledge, but still tied to in longing. We know too little, but we know too much, she tells us here, to believe with the innocence and simple faith of Leonardo. The poet, however, stands for retrenchment, for rediscovery, for reaffirmation of a whole set of values, which her minor/major literary tradition, Mennonite literature and language, supports fully in its understanding of its own territorial past and ideals.

Many examples in all three of Klassen's books of poetry support her role as standard-bearer for a territory the Mennonite community thinks it believes in and honestly reveres. We know that such a community does not exist. All territory is deterritory; all territory is reterritory. Klassen's role within the Mennonite Canadian community is to act less like a deterritorializer than like a bringer-back-into-focus of the traditional values of Mennonite spirituality. Since she is a poet, she reinstitutes the traditional values of the lyrical poetic tradition, which is equally as moralistic and anti-material in its values, though not in its habits, as Mennonite Canadian territory. Klassen teaches that each one of us would, if we only had the strength—a strength we must long for in the same way we are taught to long for the bird mother, for everything lyrical and beautiful without being able to have it—"fling yourself / and like an air-drawn eagle / fly" into the sky, closer to the sun, closer to what is good and more refined and less olfactory and tactile. Yes, once again, the writer treads on the world of touch in the attempt to fling herself ever into the sky, lead-footed as she is, away from her outrageous desires, away from her unpredictable love of pretty pupils who arrive "in white / porcelain skin. Most of [it] covered with black / leather and cloth" (9), away from what "whispers," that which "inked in delicate black / whispers" to her across great territories, that which whispers to her to come and touch, to come and taste.

From Sarah Klassen's fine lyrical poetry we move on to a storyteller who writes strong fiction not altogether unlike Klassen's in its treatment of Mennonite territory. David Elias's two books of short stories tell of a young man, Steven, raised in a rather remote part of the Pembina Hill region of southern Manitoba. The place Steven grows up in may be out of the way, but his personality and adventures seem anything but remote from the Mennonite reader's experiences.

In "Not Even the Moon," Steven finds himself hurrying to town to hang out with his new girlfriend, Marie. We know from the start that she cares less for him than the other way around. Small details, well drawn, cleverly provided, tell us that this young man lacks the dazzle that such a little beauty requires if she is to remain a kept woman. His ineptness comes home to us in the scene where he finally makes it, by dint of great effort—hitchhiking, biking and so on, since his father refuses him the use of the truck—to the diner where Marie waitresses, only to find her dallying with the town dandy and eyeing Steven with distaste.

> He sat down, leaving an empty stool between himself and the others. Nobody said anything. Marie kept staring at his shirt. He looked down at the white material and saw that it was soaked through with sweat in several places, but worse than that, the wet patches were a dirty grey colour. Maybe it was dust from the road. Or maybe he'd washed in too much of a hurry. Either way, it looked pretty awful. (*Crossing the Line* 107)

Unexpectedly, what follows this little scene, where we think we will get a common reproduction of the theme of the sassy town girl who spurns the naively hopeful country bumpkin, is instead a much darker picture of Marie in a car with Jerry heading past Steven. This car with his coy girlfriend in it occurs in his imagination only as he walks the many disappointed miles home from town.

We sense that Steven might soon suffer some sort of mental collapse, or that he must find some resolution through art for such disconnections from reality. Elias provides a disturbing magical (gothic) imagination instead of a predictably "realistic" one. This dark imagination is one of the most persuasive reasons for reading his books. Though the stories disturb our expectations for the real and the predictable, they never threaten us, nor bite from behind like dogs miscalculated as friendly.

In "The Laughter of the Devil," the first piece in *Crossing the Line,* Steven and his sister Trudy visit the zoo, where they see a hyena pacing back and forth in a cramped cage. Steven draws a sobering comparison between Trudy and the caged animal. He feels tremendous sympathy for his sister, crippled at a young age by polio, unable to participate with the other children who speedily move from one zoo-sight to another. Trudy, quiet and reticent, sits watching the hyena. She eventually breaks the silence by saying that God chose to make her an invalid to test her and that if she believes fully enough He will eventually heal her. Steven drives a wedge between himself and his sister when he asks Trudy if possibly God wanted for her to plead with Him for healing without ever intending for her to get better. In the end, however, Trudy finds the means to bind them together again, drawing strength from their difference from other people. "Trudy placed her tiny hand in Steven's. 'We're not like the others, are we?' she said" (*Crossing the Line* 11). This story, moving for the reader as an account of intense family love, also indicates the importance of the idea of the artist in Elias's work. Trudy, herself rejected, understands the difficulty of the artist's separation from others within his community, for the artist sees too much, sees too differently, to belong.

In "Hidden Places," Steven and his friend Bill, bicycling out into the Pembina Hills, find an old shack inhabited by a family new to the area. This family, hill people, poor, cruel as the parents are to their children, makes the reader think about common Tennessee hillbilly stories; makes her think about *Deliverance*. This new family turns out, ironically, to be recent immigrants from Mexico. In a climactic moment, Rudy, the young immigrant boy, who joins the lads in their wild bike rides down coulees and hills, slaps his little sister across the face and knocks her to the ground to keep her from following them. With this violence he simply repeats what he has learned at the hands of his father.

> Steven got up and walked to the window. The man was just closing the trunk and the boy was standing beside him, saying something. They separated and got into the car. When the boy said something else, the man leaned over and lashed him with the back of his hand. (*Crossing* 16)

Such tyrannical rage strikes too close to Mennonite home for comfort.

In "Crossing the Line," Steven and Bill foolishly go rafting in the icy, swollen Pembina River. What happens in this "crossing," sudden, swift, and unexpected, changes Steven's life forever. It haunts him and drives his artistic vision. The special effect of this story is its indefiniteness about what happened. The narrator, unwilling to divulge all, tells us in so many words that this event acted as a muse for him. Too important to him, too damaging to his sense of place and purpose to tell completely, it succeeds in making him a writer.

In "Egg Shells and Dragon Skin," Steven and Trudy come to know a mentally challenged vagrant named Sonny who illegally crosses the States line one misty morning. They put him up in their tree house for a few days and provide for him, bringing him food and water. He eventually shows them, in an act of tender acceptance, the prized possessions he carries in a little pouch. A few days later he disappears, only to reappear in the most unexpected way.

David Elias's two books of short stories unsettle the reader. I expected works less biting, less incisive, possibly because, in my estimation, the strength of most engaging short stories derives from their non-didactic curiosity about human life in a social context familiar to the author (arguably the product of major, lyrical inculcation in my construction). In my experience,

Mennonites in our age tend to look neither carefully nor closely at their surroundings and their relationships, unless preparing a sermon, and we know the object of their gaze then.

Elias's books, unprudish and unpreachy, focus on the imaginary world of the developing Mennonite artist. Steven, the central character in both *Crossing the Line* and *Places of Grace*, delights us with his curiosity about human life. His perceptions declare everywhere his eccentricity, his dislike of dogma, his pleasure in pleasure, and his joy with words, with love, with freedom, with independence, and so on. Sensitive, he loves his enemies, with the exception of his father, who appreciates nothing except work: work to be done, and work well done; long hours of it. Open to experiences of various kinds, biblical but in a fresh way, imaginative and adventurous, hardly interested in money as his father is, and in many ways an attractive character, Steven nevertheless hates his father with as much passion as his father loves money, penury, and hard work.

Steven despises his father's narrow views. He despises the quality of Mennonite thoughtlessness about anything except the practical; the Mennonite lack of imagination. The artist with a sensitive nature and mind, Steven dislikes the quality his people most live by: austerity. The story "The Jude" combines in one representation all these dislikable qualities, the dislikable qualities of one sort of typical twentieth century Mennonite. A fruit-selling Jew arrives every year at Steven's parents' farmyard. Each year the sounds, sights, and smells of the truck carrying its fruit draw the young boy hungrily from the house.

> The first thing I'd do when I got to the back of the truck was take a long, deep breath. This would carry the amazing mixture of fragrances that spilt out of the dark interior into my lungs— the smell of bananas and oranges, apples and pears. These sultry aromas acted like a potion that shook me out of my winter doldrums and snapped me into life. (*Places of Grace* 23)

Every year, though, as regular as clockwork, his father initiates an argument over price. Consequently, as often as not, no fruit gets bought or eaten at all and Steven feels his disappointment so intensely that he cannot forgive his father.

And that sums up most of Steven's life experiences in his

village: penury, hard work, and a group of people immune to pleasures and joys. By way of example, in "How I Crossed Over," young Steven learns some Negro gospel songs from an old South African, songs the boy instinctively knows he had been waiting to learn since the day of his birth, so alive, so joyful, they make him feel. He and his friend Bill belt out one of the bluesy tunes one day in Miss Enns's Sunday School class and are severely strapped for it by the preacher: "The preacher got very red, then, and looked over at the others. 'This is the work of the devil,' he said, 'when boys quote scripture to twist their way out of trouble.' He turned to Miss Enns and the others. 'You're excused,' he said. 'I'll handle it from here'" (*Places of Grace* 68). Everything fun is the devil in the Mennonite evangelical backwoods of Elias's tales. The stories themselves, however, by way of contrast, speak of a strange birth from such severity and frigidity. All in all, despite their subject of cultural anality, they hold out tantalizing narrative pleasures to us like "the Jude" held out oranges and apples.

One expects common realism from rural Pembina Valley writing as a rule, but instead with Elias one is treated to sting, wit, and the fantastic, all wonderful gifts. What one gets too little of, though (and which I wish writers of Mennonite stories would roll themselves in occasionally) is freedom with the body. Mennonite authors notoriously shun sex and sexuality, thinking of it as sin and bad, or bad for the reputation. Or, if they speak of bodily spragnations at all, they do so under the general rubric of "the flesh" (see Di Brandt's and Pat Friesen's poetry), that ethereal and unpalpable alternative for the entity that sweats, secretes various obvious fluids (shit, piss, pus, snot, lymph juices, and that other juice we Mennonites must not speak of), hungers suddenly and unaccountably for a quickie, and so on. They typically avoid representing the pleasuring body. Or they put sex and the body's various affects and causes of sweatiness in the wings, off stage, out of view, where they can pen away about it as if it happened without having to show it in its details. The reader knows what the cute teacher, with her hair rumpled and the top buttons of her dress undone, has been doing in the woods in "The Handshake" (*Places of Grace*) when Steven bumps into her there. Why not show it? In its entirety? We know what Bill saw in the same story, peeping through the pretty teacher's window, but we do not get to see it, left inevitably unsatisfied and arrested in our pleasures, like the man and maid on Keats's Grecian urn.

A young woman who has been writing fine poetry for many years now, merits a more comprehensive study than I can give at this time. Audrey Poetker has published a number of books of poetry, any one of which could be usefully analyzed for their "Mennonite" content, the last one no less than any of the others. Her first, *i sing for my dead in german*, won her recognition in the Manitoba and Canadian literary scene for a certain intense sexuality, as well as for its sharp criticism of Mennonites at home.

One way to begin to interpret her most recent published volume would be to think of a title for an essay one could write about it for a local literary magazine: "Old Man, Young Wife, No Children: the Suffering of the Childless in Audrey Poetker's *Making strange to yourself.*" The poetic scene of *Making strange to yourself* is a marriage relationship between a young woman and an old man. In it the reader finds a young woman who has much to say and an old man who is essentially foolish and in need of his physically young, emotionally older wife's wisdom.

> The old man strokes lightly the pink nipples of his young wife. Candles flicker as night blows into the room through the open window. Leaf shadows cluster his face. *Tell me another story*, he says, closing his Madeira eyes. The young wife sighs. If no one believes the truth, how will they believe the stories? She shivers and reaches with her thin arm to cradle her husband's hoary head against her breasts. And then she begins to speak. (untitled prelude)

The poems that follow tell this "other story" of hers, a story of wanting something that the words and mouth of her husband cannot provide, infertile as they are. She wishes for children and remains barren, too; this is the gist of all the "story" she tells him in the first part of the book. The title already prepares the reader for the subject of the barren mother. The cliché about "making strange," usually applied to infants who fear separation from their mothers and who consequently make everyone else near them except Mother intensely unwelcome, in this case appears to apply to the adult female persona of the poems. The story tells us, in fact, that not she herself but her old husband has become very strange to the young wife. The wife has begun at some point in their marriage to perceive *herself* as a child. Though physically mature and getting older, she feels bereft of the emotional possibility of becoming an adult, stuck, it seems to her, in a perpetual state of childish strangeness.

The fault lies with the husband somehow, the wife thinks. He makes love to her with average vigour and more than average interest, but he cannot fill her womb, and she is by now only mildly optimistic: "Another lover's / sperm would bore into your egg like a bee into a rose, a / pneumatic drill into oak" (10). She cannot love him fully, conscious as she is of his impotence: "His hands, reaching for my breasts, / sometimes I'm there and sometimes / I'm not there, my eyes are always / filled with tears" (13). Childless, she blames first herself, almost before she blames "him." "Your body refuses to release its eggs, it clings to them, a / jealous lover" (10). And again, self-blaming, in "After the Fall": "did you ever tell anyone that? / you spent ten woman years trying *not* to get // pregnant, and then, you couldn't with all / that trying" (7). In a highly lyrical moment, in a poem entitled "Old Man," she fantasizes about what it would be like to have married a younger man, to be a young woman, alive, lithe, hopeful, trenchant with still unproved potency and possibility, and married to a man with a "wishbone" capable of fulfilling the desire at the heart of her wish (clearly—and cleverly—shaped like a wishbone with its slender structure a miniature female legs and womb entrance): "Suppose we both were young / and the history of our hearts / was not yet sung . . . and we, we were wish // and wishbone" (14). The journey she longs to take is the journey of love and motherhood; a journey that begins in "throbbing," joyful, young experience and ends in the "sun" light of children. But, sadly, not to be for her.

She admits, in this long poetic narrative to her aging husband, to having tried other lovers, as in "Darling, the doctor is in." No sense of apology filters through these lines, only facts, only a statement of attempted child making. Finally, she imagines the "old man's" death; not maliciously, not with longing so much as with a finality of understanding. "Someday, someday too soon /

I will bury you, lover / in the clay of the great Lake Agassiz" (17). Her fear of his loss to her, however, takes the form of a comparison of children's fears at ghost stories (not unlike the apparition of stories she is telling her old husband as she lies in his arms). Her thought is not of his death but of their childlessness when he dies: "As children do with ghost stories / I scare myself with a widow's bed" (17). He will be remembered for the coarse and unhappy, for the irritating, not for fine things: "what is your old man's grief / to mine, that first day that I awaken / without your icky morning breath / and bed farts, our homely love, love?" (17).

He will be dead much sooner than she and all they will have had to show for their "love" is a shallow thrusting and a set of childless embraces adorned with his fruitless intellectualism: "How softly you quote Goethe / to me, when I am frantic with grief" (27). His mouth's pained whispering, a sign of his own grief at not being able to satisfy his ailing wife, is insignificant, as she has claimed, in contrast with her mouth's silence in the world.

> There is no child with my mouth
> how can I laugh?
> There is no child with my nose
> whom can I console?
> I am not a mother
> how can I save myself
> with my womb full of silence
> empty of desire? (25)

The set of poems that begins this book ends simply with the notes of grief, the mouth's inconsolable emptiness and silence like a childless womb.

> Nearer
> than my thoughts, moving over me
> with cruel understanding,
> you find it, heal it with your tongue
> and I cry out, cry out. (27)

Making strange to yourself is well worth reading by a general readership as well as by Mennonites, even if it is for Mennonites possibly too graphic a look at married love and loss. I recommend it to those who are not easily offended or afraid in their own lives of reading the experiences/imaginations of others. I do not think this book will harm anyone or take anything away from anyone, but instead will contribute to our culture's continued understanding of the pain and suffering of individuals in our midst. All humans in the late twentieth century, just like all humans through the ages, suffer dark losses that we hardly know how or dare to name. Poetker names her dark losses and asks us to read about them without crying foul or worse. A community is a group of people who welcome all its members, weak and strong, hurt or happy, sad or joyful, wretched or successful, with open arms and try not to name individuals out of existence. By this I mean that a community tries not to force all members to conform because if it attempts that, it loses the possibility of understanding the complex nature of life itself. Poetker's book, painful material for some, is worth reading because of its poetic treatment of afflictions common to members of the Mennonite (and all other) communities.

Another recently successful Mennonite writer, Miriam Toews, who deserves a wide readership, writes like T.S. Eliot, in the objective correlative style I considered in Pat Friesen's poem "bluebottle." She writes, therefore, in a style that cares little for presenting herself, the clever author, but only a hard, clear image of the subject at hand, being first a modernist and not a minor writer. The objective correlative method presents an idea entirely concretely without abstraction, showing instead of telling. This mode of writing literature (or philosophy or religion, though seldom adopted by these last two disciplines— Nietzsche's *The Genealogy of Morals* is an exception) is *the* highpoint of Western literary practice and represents an ambitious goal on Toews's part. Nothing is more sophisticated and, consequently, more a product of ages of the development of literary conventions than imagism in lyrical poetry, and "the objective correlative" in poetic and narrative genres. For that reason, only the mastery of this method and the deliberate subversion of it by and after such mastery would be "minor" writing; that, or the happy bumbling and so accidental approximation of this method by a hopeful writer. In other words, accidental or deliberate minor writing both subvert the major literature system. Toews's subversion of the major, when it occurs at all, is accidental.

Miriam Toews is a committed practitioner of the "objective correlative." Much as in "The Lovesong of J. Alfred Prufrock," where Eliot gave us the hard, clear character type of the foolish, professorial lover deeply afraid of women but fantasizing about being heroic enough to have the women notice him and love him, so Toews presents us with a crystalline character type, in *A Boy of Good Breeding*, of a Winnipeg welfare mom. The protagonist's boyfriend and father of her child has left them in the lurch. This mother suffers less than welfare mothers typically would in stories by less capable writers. In fact, she seems intelligently at home with her lot. She comfortably swears, uses the Anglo-Saxon for vulva and penis and breast and sexual intercourse, lives with her parents in rural Manitoba when she wishes to get away from the *ennui* of the city, and in a hundred ways shows the reader how uniquely twentieth century her worldview is. She is a marvellously "free" character, ethically self-determined, morally unbound by old evangelical Mennonite religious bonds, and able to relate to youth in the late nineties.

This creation of a credible late-twentieth-century character without the moral, religious, political, and social "hang-ups" of the generations before (fifties, sixties, seventies, and eighties) indicates less that Toews manages to forge a minor character powerfully subversive of the old symbolic, but that she writes exceptionally well in the very conventions that most clearly represent the major. Toews's other works, too, master the major instead of subverting it. *Swing Low* is a strong example. It tells the story of Melvin Toews, Steinbach schoolteacher *extraordinaire*, who lives in a personal depression of such severity that he commits suicide a few years after his retirement. The reader hears very little of Miriam Toews's abstract thoughts about depression or fatherhood and so on, but sees only evocative images, and the accurate, concrete presentation of the exact details of the self-indulgence and banality of the severely manic-depressive.

Mel Toews, the schoolteacher, now late in his life and in the hospital suffering from a severe bout of manic depression, writes a series of lists and details important to his past. These details or little memories include the story of his first meeting with his wife-to-be, Elvira, in grade four. In an early memory, he describes gregarious, popular Elvira waltzing down the aisle past him, shy, timid, forgettable Mel. In an act of sudden, bad bravery, he "stabs" Elvira with his compass.

> Speaking of school days, I shamefully recall the day I stabbed Elvira with the sharp end of my compass. I suppose I was seven or eight and just beginning to have feelings, unknowable, inexpressible feelings of . . . love? No. Infatuation? I'm not sure, even today, what you would call that vague need for approval from the opposite sex. (47-48)

Shyly self-conscious, Mel, telling his own story, focusses on his desire for approval from the opposite sex. Sounds to me a lot like Prufrock. But never mind. Mel's methods are never as timid as he likes to make them seem, and as the women in his life believe. He is quite aggressive in his wallflower ways.

> In any case, I wanted Elvira to like me, and in my mind, though not consciously at the time, I thought I would spur that approval on by . . . stabbing her? No, not the actual stabbing, but the display of nerve and timing and discernment (I chose her, after all) that the stabbing act required (I got her in the rear end as she walked past my desk). (48)

Although he would like to call what he did "stabbing"—the histrionics at the heart of manic-depression precisely suggested by Toews, understated—he draws no blood, having just neatly pricked her enough to make her say ouch and hit him. Her reaction starts something between them that over the years grows finally into "love," and eventually leads to their unlikely marriage. Elvira has never known seriously sneaky ways; she has never had to practise secrecy and manipulation, being smart, lively, bright, outgoing, and familiar enough with the world to live in it with poise and "loudness." She is sent to kindergarten at the age of two, bored with just sitting at home (the opposite of Mel, who prefers home on all occasions). Elvira, before Mel, is well adjusted.

> Somewhere in my collection there is a school photograph of our kindergarten class. Elvira is wearing a short brown dress, thick knit stockings, sturdy leather shoes, and,

> unfortunately, two fierce braids (I loathe braids) and is sitting on the grass in the front row with her legs spread, her elbows out like two handles on a teacup, her neck craned forward and her face jutting towards the camera. She is taking up far too much room (in the photo her head is twice the size of everyone else's), and the girls on either side of her are squished in and trying to hold their own for the shot. She has that expression on her face that seems to say, I've just done something extremely naughty and I am as pleased as punch about it. (48-49)

The protagonist observes the proprieties (she is "pleased as punch"), banal, stupid, niggling, a milksop; the subject of his manipulations is actually accustomed to being naughty, someone who would never develop a mastery of the conventions of clichés that in English say the same old without saying anything. The protagonist masters these clichés, empty as he is of open personal naughtiness or subversion of any sort. The victim, the author implies through ironies in the text, masters proprieties, decorum, niceties and timidity, whining for his public persona and never the pleasures of rebellion. The strong person, lover of her own mischievous freedom, is the real victim-who-does-not-think-of-herself-as-a-victim because she is strong. She becomes a victim, aware of her sad demise of freedom, life and love at the hands of the manipulative one only after decades of being controlled while pacifically loving the unempathetic one. That Mel is not interested in love but in approval is evident in the earlier quotation. That Elvira is long-suffering is evident in a following passage. He is already hospitalized in his late life, he has a doctor's appointment, he has forgotten the order of shaving and appointments, and has just shaved after seeing the doctor. Elvira says as much to him, gentle and loving as always.

> It was only after the appointment, as I stood at the bathroom sink, razor in hand, gazing sadly at my foamy reflection, that Elvira gently reminded me of the sequence. Mel, she said in a soft whisper all empty of hope, you might have shaved before the appointment. (46)

Elvira has been "duped" into marrying this self-doubting plotter. And what a plotter he is. But that is the matter of the entire book, showing the reader the complexity of his con artistry with extremely careful lists of details and memories presented in the most exacting way. It is not a matter to prove by citing an example or two here. The general method, I can say, of this objective presentation, is established by the examples above, however. The important fact is that Mel, first-person narrator, is not reliable in the telling of his own story. A secondary, "authorial" version of his story becomes the centre of Toews's account, and that story tells the reader what a selfish character Mel was in the eyes of his patient wife and his slightly less patient female children. *Swing Low,* then, in short, is the masterful, objective presentation of the character of the manic-depressive who seems to be the victim of his disease but who controls with ferocious banality the comings, goings, emotions, loves, lives, pleasures, freedoms, and other personal belongings of all the members of his family. With grace and love, Miriam Toews quietly tells the story of the terror within a family of the iron hand of psychopathic control, which rules through weakness, to the point even of self-destruction when the circle of his control starts to disintegrate, as all psychopaths' control inevitably does after about thirty or forty years.

The Mennonite writers considered in this chapter hold in common the fact that they are voices for the territory within whose borders they were raised, and whose rules and codes they understand and represent. Each of them speaks the politics (codes and rules) of the Mennonite Canadian group, and, in the sense that this group is one among many gathered at the borders of the dominant English territory, we may humorously, but also accurately, think of them as surplus at the English border, as writing excess, as governed by a desire to be heard and accepted by the naturalized citizens of the English territory. "Minor" writers of English, they speak the language of authenticity, of sincerity, of clear political statement. Paradoxically, however, they must use whatever means necessary to cross into the territory that dominates the rules and codes that accept or reject writing and writers. Sincere, intense, self-exposing, these recent Mennonite writers also walk the tightrope of compromise, practising the arts of charm and infiltration, intending to be among those selected for immigration hearings from among the surplus of groups gathered at the border.

8.

Knocking about the Border:
Mennonite Writing at the *Gjrentz*

I have analyzed the work of various important contributors to the body of Mennonite Canadian literature. The critical theory that guided my study has been mainly Gilles Deleuze and Félix Guattari's idea of the revolutionary value of minor writing—how minor writing deterritorializes major writing by calling for a return of a territory it assumes exists somewhere in some form or other, whether, as in Sarah Klassen's case, a Mennonite territory of ethical and political attitudes largely identical to those of high modernism, or, in Di Brandt's case, a non-Mennonite territory in which women find out from reading her work that they were once powerful beings whom men had to deal with seriously and who now, though made powerless by patriarchal violence, are beginning to show evidence of a sort of female progress back to a state they once enjoyed thousands of years ago. All the writers appraised in this book have, in dealing with the problem of Mennonite Canadian territory, written against major literary conventions. Some have written in greater complicity with major conventions while others have almost done away with the marks of, and so most effectively subverted and changed, major literature.

The individual and collective accomplishments of the writers have suggested themselves in the course of my study. Each of the Mennonite Canadian writers has lent a distinctive voice to the deterritorialization of major English territory within the Canadian context, as well as to the deterritorialization and reterritorialization of his or her own group in new literary space, reinforcing what he or she deemed valuable of an old territory, a territory which is by necessity textual. All the writers have had some things in common. Each has contributed to a collective or reterritorializing voice that has shaped and will continue to shape a future Mennonite Canadian group with identifiable social material formations.

Rudy Wiebe's novel *Peace Shall Destroy Many* represents the beginning of Mennonite fiction writing interesting to a broad English-speaking audience. Considering the problem of how his work fits the definition of minor literature, we need to ask two questions: 1) How is it political and how does it carry community values? 2) In what specific ways does it subvert major literature? It acts politically by narratively announcing that especially three institutions determine Mennonite Canadian community: the church, the state, and the artist. The first two operate hummingly to direct the community and lead it as long as it is not in crisis, but eventually a crisis develops around the very lies that church and state tell in order to convince the social group that it is a permanent and unchanging entity. When this evasion becomes impossible to be held up as truth or reality any longer, and individuals in the community begin to rebel against the established leadership and its discourse of permanence, then the third institution starts to affect the group's body by writing a story of its political and ethical formations. This artistic story contains a strong indication of "honest" self-surveillance, which shows the group both what is wrong with its social formations and how to change these formations in order to learn from the lesson of its own blindness and reconstitute itself again as a believing community. This believing reconstitution is a *believing* entity in that the community finds new fictions to tell itself about permanence which will allow it to inhere as a group once again for the foreseeable future, inhere and remain assured of the goodness and badness of sets of things, of the importance of the effort to unify what is disparate, of the predictable dualities that make up all that is textual.

Wiebe's novels infiltrate and subvert the cherished beliefs of major English literature. They subvert by showing their own insides, turning themselves inside out, that is, so what is usually not seen by major literature of the social corpus now is made visible and plain to see by minor literature. In concrete terms, Wiebe's novels show Mennonite politics and community values interacting with the less plain politics of the Canadian nation. This narrative self-exposure of politics and values challenges the exclusivist values and politics of the dominant, major literary group. Minor self-exposure subverts by showing the major group that it too is politically determined, and that politics is constructed, not originary, not permanent or eternal. *Peace Shall Destroy Many's* struggle with the questions of conscientious objection and relations to Aboriginal people, with the exposure of the hypocrisy and violence at the heart of these formations, forces major readers of this text to change in their self-understanding, as minor readers of it are forced to do as well.

Thus, in the case of *Peace Shall Destroy Many*, the hero Thom comes to symbolic blows with Deacon Block, local theocrat, when he fights Herb Unger, himself a renegade Mennonite who represents Mennonitism turned nihilistic (utter individualism, that is), and in doing so, and doing so for all intents and purposes as an artist, he first thinks through Block's failing community logic, and then, by resistance to this hypocritical discourse, by telling its story in the novel, begins the reconstruction of Mennonites according to codes that will better understand the Mennonite Canadian community's relationship with their Aboriginal neighbours as well as their inadequate view of peace and nonresistance, the cornerstone of Mennonite doctrine.

Armin Wiebe's contribution to the body of Mennonite Canadian minor writing seems more difficult to pinpoint than Rudy Wiebe's or Patrick Friesen's. Among his three novels, his first, *The Salvation of Yasch Siemens*, stands as the most accessible and important for the questions concerned with Mennonite Canadian territoriality. In a fascinating inversion, which reveals the hypocrisy at the heart of Mennonite Canadian rural life, Armin Wiebe presents first a convincing account of Mennonite social material existence, and then a version of their existence which *affirms* the facile spirituality by which many Mennonite

Canadians live and think. Wiebe's rambunctious materialism delights the reader and endears to him the Mennonite lifestyle. The book's final spiritual resolution, however, disaffects the reader and shows him how spirituality is a constructed corpus of qualities that the individual Mennonite must believe if he is to survive politically and communally. The upshot of this dramatic reversal of perspectives effectively demonstrates the hypocrisy by which Mennonite Canadians live. This hypocrisy consists of an inculcated acceptance of lies as truth, of a serious simplification of the complexity of desiring-production (a technical term of Gilles Deleuze's for the material, nomadic life) into desire for a heaven that substitutes for desire and pleasure on earth. Lying to themselves about the bounty of heaven and the joy of the postponement of material pleasures, Mennonites live according to an official, institutional agenda, which requires such lies of them. They are among the most material of all peoples or groups imaginable in their eating, drinking, pleasuring habits, but they are also among the most self-deceiving about their indulgences.

Pat Friesen's poetry tells thematically of the difficulty of becoming a poet in a Mennonite Canadian social milieu, and it tells stylistically and thematically of the struggle, relevant to the becoming-poet conflict, of writing a poetry that thinks the Canadian prairie when all indicators point him toward writing lyrical and non-thinking poetry. The first difficulty finds expression throughout Friesen's works in this way: it brings the religious pressure to accept the language of spiritual asceticism and biblical Christianity, as Mennonite Canadians have transmitted it, into constant contact with another more material and "embodied" side of Mennonite life. In this space of intimate contact, Peter teaches his brother Johann, in the course of the events in *The Shunning*, that the Mennonite world of food and drink and lovemaking is more reliable and valuable, that is, more honest, than its world of high conformity represented by the church brotherhood's requirements of obedience to accept various doctrines it has inherited from a territorial past, which no longer has, and possibly never had any, life-sustaining power in the New World. As for the second function of the poet, Friesen constantly juxtaposes a material aesthetic with a lyrical one, being efficient in the latter, and gradually becoming more efficient at the former. The most effective quality of Friesen's body of poetry might well be said to be precisely this aspect of his growth as a poet. Writing with great competence as a lyric poet, he yet presents much of his work without lyrical apparati and techniques, thrusts to the foreground the very problem of the hegemony of lyrical poetics. He foregrounds, in other words, the *problem* of lyricism. He foregrounds the lyric's easy and facile domination over local poetics, and by writing a "waiting" aesthetics alongside the "always-already complete" lyrical poetics, he offers a forceful critique of both social and aesthetic indifference to and fear within the new land, the Canadian prairies. The poet serves the purposes of being a spokesman for a new poetics in a new land: he speaks against coming to the prairies armed with all the spiritual bric-a-brac of an outmoded eurocentric and classical spirituality, and he speaks for a new spiritual social materialism, which waits for the land to speak to those newcomers it has welcomed and to teach them in this waiting to abandon old formations and learn to enjoy the gifts of new ones there in abundance for those neither too afraid nor too proud to accept its gifts. The poet's duty, as Friesen's work teaches, is to be the voice of the conflict between European arrogance and tyranny (that is, fear), and the new land's patient, material goodness.

Of Di Brandt's many distinctive contributions, the one I have chosen to discuss is her problematizing the question of gender among Mennonite Canadians. She has chosen to step outside official circles—such as the church, the traditional Mennonite family, and other constants governing various social formations and their moral foundation—to critique Mennonites and others from, essentially, the site of general deterritorialization and non-community, the city. From here she argues that women are victims of male violence and need to find the strength to rediscover their past power, now unfortunately in long and terrible decline. In this present state, women, who once were not afraid of anything, empowered as they were by "mother blood" (*Jerusalem, beloved* 60), now fear spiders. Despite her present debilitating fears, woman continues to love, both the earth and the children she bears. It is through love, and especially through the writing of love by poets such as herself, that women can begin the eradication of millennia-old male fear, hatred, and danger to the earth. The main thrust of Brandt's writing, the main thrust of this new female power, is for the daughters of the world's (and especially the Mennonite world's) birthing mothers. Hearing her story, seeing her courage in her personal struggle, they too will become strong enough to join the resistance against disempowerment, Brandt implies.

Part of the great struggle for Brandt and for mothers is the loss of identity. The mother in Western literature is an absence. She has not been inscribed and so has yet to be constructed as a subject. Her individuation process requires of her that she become nothing; that she give up power so that the daughters who follow her can take over without having to remain under her shadow. This form of individuation seems very Frygian to me, the daughters overthrowing their mothers in order to take power themselves. It represents a reversal of Freudian Oedipal family politics, matriarchal as it is, but disquietingly still in Freudian and archetypal terms. For Brandt, birthing children is the great female experience. Birthing a child effectively separates her from males. They never can know the "self-birth" of giving birth to a child and giving it suck (*Jerusalem, beloved*), and this takes a woman beyond all male experience. Effectively, giving birth to a child represents giving birth to herself—individuation from the male.

Right at this juncture, Brandt's work and thought connect with the Mennonite Canadian community. The language of Mennonite Canadians perpetrates female victimization by male victimizers.

> i stole the language
> of their kings and queens,
>
> but i didn't bow down to it,
> i didn't become a citizen. (*mother, not mother* 30)

The greatest problem the female poet faces in her Mennonite group is the force that silences her. Females, separated from their codependency on their violent male Mennonite perpetrators, feel a longing for acceptance and company. The key, as Brandt sees it, is for the female poet to continue to resist, despite her longing and loneliness, and eventually her resistance to forces of silence will result in new and delightful singing, and the end of

Mennonite Canadian's "terrible God," whose very language hurts the innocent. That old despair and the struggle to overcome it. That old writing from despair.

More than ever before, writing from despair characterizes the mindset of the young Canadian writer. David Bergen, in *Sitting Opposite My Brother*, along with Sandra Birdsell, Pat Friesen, and others, write as if despair were a new phenomenon, as if the exhausted voice were an original and exciting one.

The novels and short stories of Sandra Birdsell accomplish something extraordinary in minor writing. They present a subjectivity constructed out of an intimate acquaintance with two clashing territories, the Aboriginal Canadian and the Mennonite Canadian. The group dynamics of these two share a long mutual history and kinship. Ever since "settling" this land, Mennonites have acted as if the Aboriginal owner of the land were not the owner of the land. In other words, the Mennonite Canadian has had to live hypocritically in relation to the Aboriginal from whom he effectively stole land. As she grew more aware of his theft as a theft, she had to become more wily in her denial of the theft in order to live with herself, and to keep up the appearances of believing in a territory that had its taproot still nestled in the not very nourishing spiritual-intellectual reservoirs of Germany, Russia, and all the West's classical traditions. Birdsell does not discuss this tension in its particularities, but she assumes it. Where Rudy Wiebe tells all, opens up to the reader the precise politics of hypocritical, pioneering, Mennonite Canada, Birdsell draws us portraits of individual Mennonites and Aboriginal people, co-existing in Agassiz, Manitoba, who are fully deterritorialized from their spiritual-political territories and who await a saviour who will never come because they are too blind to see him, or her, as *The Missing Child* sees it. Blindness is a form of deterritorialization. Mennonites and Aboriginal people in Canada are blind to the power around them to hope and love. What happens to the individual subjects, then, is that in their blindness, they see only themselves, in classical high modernist tradition, and so they cannot belong to any group except the major group of all the alienated. The alienated are those literary figures who are drawn by authors of the school of Eliot and Pound as having no ability to see the meaning and goodness around them. They are necessarily in despair. These fictional figures always approach a reterritorializing situation and then fail to make good of it. They opt, psychically and spiritually, at each moment of choice, for a despairing, material world. They fail at each step of the way. Their failure is the failure to see the possibilities of pleasure and joy in the material. This is the dilemma of Maurice and Mika in *Night Travellers*, of Albert, Rosella, and Minnie in *The Missing Child*, and of Amy, Jill, Pyotr, and others in *The Chrome Suite*. In each case the individual deterritorialized subjects, Mennonite and Aboriginal often, are left entirely alone, belonging to no group, convinced of nothing but the hopelessness of their efforts to belong. The value of Birdsell's fiction to the question of Mennonite Canadian and Aboriginal Canadian territory is that in her extreme deterritorialization of these groups from the possibility of finding meaning in old notions of territory, she paves the way for a future reterritorialization based on non-territorial, and so material, possibilities.

John Weier, Sarah Klassen, Lois Braun, Miriam Toews, David Bergen, Delbert Plett, Al Reimer, Audrey Poetker, and David Elias (and various other writers I have not discussed in this book) also significantly contribute to the overall picture of Mennonite Canadian minor literature. Weier's work resists the territorial Mennonite metaphysical text that makes of each moment of speech and writing an opportunity to insert a superior divine being into material being. Weier writes about the subject and his material world as if it were fully constructed. His reterritorializing contribution comes from his willingness to write the story of the Mennonite diaspora without affirming, as Armin Wiebe does in his fiction, the particular anti-materialism Mennonites have traditionally assiduously fostered, nay, evangelized.

Sarah Klassen is a political voice for Mennonite Canadian territory. She does not deterritorialize or unsettle fixed beliefs and dispositions. Her efforts typically show how able a lyricist she is and reaffirm the values and political positions of her Mennonite community. Klassen seems to see nothing amiss, nothing unsettling, about the current relation of Mennonites to the material world around them.

Lois Braun, on the other hand, sees much amiss. Her revolutionary efforts take place in the sexual field. Her female protagonists need to escape from some sort of condition. The reasons are never very plain—the escape never clearly pointed out to be an escape from what. Various indicators in the texts, however, show through close reading a restlessness with heterosexual relations. Braun effectively deterritorializes Mennonite heterosexual metaphysics by showing us, through the assiduous literary critic who pursues textual clues with enough care, that women are much more interesting to women than men are. This is the case, at least, in the fictional worlds Braun creates, and does not necessarily mean that Braun would have no other worlds before her. Any attack on Mennonite Canadian sexuality is an attack on Mennonite Canadian territory. The specific nature or character of a reterritorialization resulting from such a sexual attack as Braun's, if it was a successful one, is hard to imagine. What would a non-heterosexual Mennonite Canadian reterritory look like? It is impossible to imagine. What would a material Mennonite Canadian reterritory be like?

Each writer discussed in this book contributes a great deal to particular reterritorializations of the Mennonite Canadian group subject. Each writer tackles the problem of being a voice for her community's values and politics in a unique way. Presumably, each writer to come from this dynamic and changing Mennonite Canadian territory will have her own revolutionary turf, his own bone to pick with the inflexibility of Mennonite Canadian territoriality. The minor quality of a writer is that quality that sees major textuality within his own ranks, and, attacking there, reduces it by enlarging it. The major is made minor by the minor's attack itself. Revolution always happens from within the ranks. Mennonite Canadian territory looses its hegemonic hold more with each minor text written. All (re)territories do that steadily, wax and wane, grow and decline, sometimes with imperceptible slowness, sometimes too quickly for the recording eye to see. Capitalism sees to that, but that is another story.

Much as Di Brandt's expectations will not be met by the feminist revolution, or by a revolution she instigates with her poems, Birdsell's alienated Mennonite Aboriginal Canadian subject is that only in her text, and Pat Friesen's lyrical/material poetic subject is only one small flutter of change in the whole picture of Mennonite life. Yet, this small flutter is such a potent wind that all of Mennonite Canadian territory eventually shifts and adjusts its vision in order to arrive at a set of temporary values that it can claim are permanent. The reminders of various individual writers, that the territory is a reterritory, stampedes Mennonite subjectivity toward some sort of abyss, some sort of terrible ocean in which it seems about to drown: the books of Birdsell, Friesen, the two Wiebes, and Brandt each bring the Mennonite group subject face to face with the ocean of his, of her, lies (permanences). Each time, however, thanks to the very Being of revolution—and being particular now, thanks to the complicity of the revolutionary, minor texts—the community walks dry shod over to a new land through what should have drowned it (see the last lines of Eliot's "Prufrock"). It walks calmly over to a new land, carrying with it all the names of the old land, plus the titles of the new and dangerous minor texts. To recapitulate and generalize, change (de- and re-territory, or Time in Heidegger's sense) is the prerequisite of Being. Permanence (territory) is the built-in hypocrisy of Being. "Man would sooner have the void for his purpose than be void of purpose . . . ." The minor hates all major languages; as Deleuze has said in *Kafka*, the minor loves speed, loves change, knows change intimately; the minor loves change but hates permanence. Being is the major undergoing change. The writing of Mennonites in Canada is a milling at the border of English, a surplus that changes itself and what it touches by its very being-there. Mennonite Canadian writing is a surplus (excessive, clamouring, busy, sometimes very humorous in its clever struggles to belong) because it participates in the attempt of all the other groups' texts, by hook or by crook, to the consternation of major English "border patrols," to infiltrate the socio-economic formations of English territory.

Low German Translation of the Excerpt from
Killing The Shamen as Printed on the Cover
Translated by Douglas Reimer

Thomas Fiddler: Aus Notleshveen Shteit Zeedvies noch laved, kunn een mensh den aundren mett fliekjes doot moake. Notleshveen ess sehja, sehja shtoijk, oba hee baudat tjehnem neemols ohnen grund. Vann eena vaut jehjen ahm oda siene tjinja deit, dann sheckt Notleshveen daut selvsje trigg noh demjanjen.

Enn dee tiet aus Notleshveen laved, saje dee menshe foake Windigo mank ehnt.

Too disse tiet kaume menshe enn disse jehjent (Windy Lake) fon Lake of White Pine Narrows, Red Lake, enn manchmol troffe see dee menshe fon Windy Lake. Dee menshe fon Lake of White Pine Narrows (Lac Seul) vere sehja shlajcht. Disse menshe haude nich fehl, bloos flintpulva, flinte, aixte enn shvehfels vaut see fon dee James Bay jehjent jetjrehje haude.

Eene somma laved een maun fon White Pine Narrows dicht bie Notleshveen, enn diss maun jing mett seene fruh enn tjinja jehjre. Notleshveen sach dissen maun fon siene jacht trig kohme enn hee tjikjt too aus diss maun sien canoe laddich mewk. Notleshveen docht diss maun haud een moose jetjrehje, enn hee hoped hee vudd ahm vaut fleesh jehve. Aus Notleshveen tootjickt, sach hee dissen maun vaut fon sien canoe rutnehme, daut via gauns bedajkt, enn hee docht daut via moose fleesh. Oba daut via nich fleesh, daut via sien tjint vaut jeshtorve via aus hee fuat via biem jehjre. Dee maun via sehja doll aus hee daut hiad; doll ehva Notleshveen.

Works Cited

Arnold, Matthew. "From Culture and Anarchy." *The Norton Anthology of English Literature.* Seventh Edition. The Major Authors. Ed. M.H. Abrams. New York: Norton, 2001.

Bergen, David. *A Year of Lesser,* Toronto: HarperCollins, 1996.

_____. *See the Child,* Toronto: HarperFlamingoCanada, 1999.

_____. *Sitting Opposite My Brother.* Winnipeg: Turnstone Press, 1993.

Birdsell, Sandra. *The Chrome Suite.* Toronto: McClelland & Stewart, 1992.

_____. *The Missing Child.* Toronto: Lester & Orpen Dennys, 1989.

_____. *Night Travellers.* Winnipeg: Turnstone Press, 1982.

Brandt, Diana. *Agnes in the sky.* Winnipeg: Turnstone Press, 1990.

_____. *Jerusalem, beloved.* Winnipeg: Turnstone Press, 1996.

_____. *mother, not mother.* Stratford: The Mercury Press, 1992.

_____. *Questions i asked my mother.* Winnipeg: Turnstone Press, 1987.

_____. *Wild Mother Dancing: Maternal Narrative in Canadian Literature.* Winnipeg: University of Manitoba Press, 1993.

Braun, Lois. *The Montreal Cats.* Winnipeg: Turnstone Press, 1995.

_____. *The Pumpkin-Eaters.* Winnipeg: Turnstone Press, 1990.

_____. *A Stone Watermelon.* Winnipeg: Turnstone Press, 1986.

Buckler, Ernest. *The Mountain and the Valley.* Toronto: McClelland & Stewart, 1989, 1961.

Coleridge, Samuel Taylor. "The Rime of the Ancient Mariner." *The Norton Anthology of English Literature.* Seventh Edition. The Major Authors. Ed. M.H. Abrams. New York: Norton, 2001.

Defoe, Daniel. *Robinson Crusoe.* Ed. Michael Shinagel. New York: Norton, 1975.

Deleuze, Gilles and Claire Parnet. *Dialogues.* Trans. Hugh Tomlinson and Barbara Habberjam. New York: Columbia University Press, 1987.

Deleuze, Gilles and Félix Guattari. *Anti-Oedipus: Capitalism and Schizophrenia.* Trans. Robert Hurley, Mark Seem and Helen R. Lane. London: Athlone Press, 1984.

_____. *Kafka: Toward a Minor Literature.* Trans. Dana Polan. Minneapolis: University of Minnesota Press, 1986.

Dryden, John. "Mac Flecknoe." *The Norton Anthology of English Literature.* Seventh Edition. The Major Authors. Ed. M.H. Abrams. New York: Norton, 2001.

Elias, David. *Crossing the Line.* Victoria: Orca Book Publishers, 1992.

_____. *Places of Grace.* Regina: Coteau Books, 1997.

Eliot, T.S. "The Lovesong of J. Alfred Prufrock." *The Norton Anthology of English Literature.* Seventh Edition. The Major Authors. Ed. M.H. Abrams. New York: Norton, 2001.

_____. "The Waste Land." *The Norton Anthology of English Literature.* Seventh Edition. The Major Authors. Ed. M.H. Abrams. New York: Norton, 2001.

Fiddler, Chief Thomas and James R. Stevens. *Killing The Shamen.* Moonbeam: Penumbra Press, 1985.

Freud, Sigmund. *Art and Literature: Jensen's Gravida, Leonardo Da Vinci, and Other Works.* Trans. James Strachey. London: Penguin, 1990.

Friesen, Patrick. *bluebottle.* Winnipeg: Turnstone Press, 1978.

_____. *the lands i am.* Winnipeg: Turnstone Press, 1976.

_____. *The Shunning.* Winnipeg: Turnstone Press, 1980.

_____. *Unearthly Horses.* Winnipeg: Turnstone Press, 1984.

Heidegger, Martin. *What Is Called Thinking.* Trans. J. Glenn Gray. New York: Harper & Row, 1968.

King, Thomas. *Green Grass, Running Water.* Toronto: HarperPerennial, 1994.

_____. *Medicine River.* Markham: Viking, 1990.

Klassen, Sarah. *Violence and Mercy.* Windsor: Netherlandic Press, 1991.

Kroetsch, Robert. *Completed Field Notes: The Long Poems of Robert Kroetsch.* Toronto: McClelland & Stewart, 1989.

_____. *The Lovely Treachery of Words.* Ed. Shirley C. Neuman and Robert Wilson. Edmonton: NeWest Press, 1982.

_____. *What the Crow Said.* Toronto: General Publishing, 1978.

Lawrence, D.H. "The Horse-Dealer's Daughter." *The Norton Anthology of English Literature.* Seventh Edition. The Major Authors. Ed. M.H. Abrams. New York: Norton, 2001.

Lyotard, Jean François. *Heidegger and "the jews."* Trans. Andreas Michel and Mark Roberts. Minneapolis: University of Minnesota Press, 1990.

Miller, Arthur. *The Crucible.* New York: The Viking Press, 1972.

Milton, John. "Comus." *Complete Poems and Major Prose.* Ed. Merritt Y. Hughes. New York: Odyssey, 1957.

_____. *Paradise Lost. The Norton Anthology of English Literature.* Seventh Edition. The Major Authors. Ed. M.H. Abrams. New York: Norton, 2001.

Nabokov, Vladimir Vladimirovich. *Lolita.* New York: Putnam, 1955.

Nietzsche, Friedrich. *The Birth of Tragedy and The Genealogy of Morals.* Trans. Francis Golffing. New York: Doubleday, 1956.

Plett, Delbert. *Sarah's Prairie.* Winnipeg: Windflower Communications, 1995.

Poetker, Audrey. *i sing for my dead in german.* Winnipeg: Turnstone, 1986.

_____. *Making strange to yourself.* Winnipeg: Turnstone, 1999.

Pope, Alexander. *The Dunciad, Variorum. With Prolegomena of Scriblerus.* Menston: The Scholar Press, 1968.

Reimer, Al. *My Harp is Turned to Mourning.* Winnipeg: Hyperion Press, 1985.

Shakespeare, William. *Hamlet. The Complete Works of Shakespeare.* Revised. Eds. Hardin Craig and David Bevington. Glenview: Scott, Foresman and Company, 1973.

_____. *The Tempest. The Complete Works of Shakespeare.* Revised. Eds. Hardin Craig and David Bevington. Glenview: Scott, Foresman and Company, 1973.

_____. *Twelfth Night. The Complete Works of Shakespeare.* Revised. Eds. Hardin Craig and David Bevington. Glenview: Scott, Foresman and Company, 1973.

Shelley, Mary Wollstonecraft. *Frankenstein; or The Modern Prometheus.* London: Toronto: J.M. Dent & Sons, 1933.

Slipperjack, Ruby. *Honour the Sun*. Winnipeg: Pemmican, 1987.

Tennyson, Alfred Lord. "The Lady of Shalott." *The Norton Anthology of English Literature*. Seventh Edition. The Major Authors. Ed. M.H. Abrams. New York: Norton, 2001.

Toews, Miriam. *A Boy of Good Breeding*. Toronto: Stoddart, 1998.

_____. *Swing Low: a Life*. Toronto: Stoddart, 2000.

Volosinov, V.N. *Freudianism: A Marxist Critique*. Trans. I.R. Titunik. Ed. Neal H. Bruss. New York: Academic Press, 1976.

Wheeler, Jordon. *Brothers in Arms*. Winnipeg: Pemmican, 1989.

Weier, John. *Steppe: A Novel*. Saskatoon: Thistledown Press, 1995.

Wiebe, Armin. *Murder in Gutenthal: A Schneppa Kjnals Mystery*. Winnipeg: Turnstone Press, 1991.

_____. *The Salvation of Yasch Siemens*. Winnipeg: Turnstone Press, 1984.

_____. *The Second Coming of Yeeat Shpanst*. Winnipeg: Turnstone Press, 1995.

Wiebe, Rudy. *A Discovery of Strangers*. Toronto: A.A. Knopf Canada, 1994.

_____. *Peace Shall Destroy Many*. Toronto: McClelland & Stewart, 1962.

_____. *The Scorched Wood People*. Toronto: McClelland & Stewart, 1977.

_____. *The Temptations of Big Bear*. Toronto: McClelland & Stewart, 1973.

Yoder, Joseph W. *Rosanna of the Amish*. Centennial Edition. Waterloo: Herald, 1995.